Harry S. Truman, the State of Israel,
and the Quest for Peace in the Middle East

Harry S. Truman, the State of Israel, and the QUEST for PEACE in the MIDDLE EAST

Proceedings of a Conference held at the
Harry S. Truman Research Institute for
the Advancement of Peace,
Hebrew University, Jerusalem,
29 May 2008

edited by
MICHAEL J. DEVINE

Truman State University Press

Cover design: Katie Best
Type: MinionPro © Adobe Systems Inc.; Myriad Pro © Adobe Systems Inc.
Printed by: Sheridan Books, Ann Arbor, Michigan USA

Library of Congress Cataloging-in-Publication Data

Harry S. Truman, the state of Israel, and the quest for peace in the Middle East :
proceedings of a conference held at the Harry S. Truman Research Institute for the
Advancement of Peace, Hebrew University, Jerusalem, 29 May 2008 / Michael J. Divine,
ed.
        p. cm.
Includes bibliographical references and index.
ISBN 978-1-935503-00-2 (hardback : alk. paper)
1. Truman, Harry S., 1884–1972—Congresses. 2. Truman, Harry S., 1884–1972—Relations
with Jews—Congresses. 3. United States—Foreign relations—Israel—Congresses.
4. Israel—Foreign relations—United States—Congresses. 5. Palestine—History—Partition,
1947—Congresses. 6. Presidents—United States—Biography—Congresses. I. Divine,
Michael J.
E814.H339 2009
973.918092—dc22

2009027161

The 40th anniversary events at the Harry S. Truman Research Institute for the Advancement of Peace, the Hebrew University of Jerusalem, were funded by the Mandel Foundation, Barbara Mandel, vice chairman.

CONTENTS

Session 3
Why Did President Truman Support
the Establishment of the State of Israel?

PREFACE

Haim D. Rabinowitch

When it opened its doors in 1968, the Harry S. Truman Research Institute for the Advancement of Peace enjoyed the personal authorization and endorsement of former United States president Harry S. Truman. The Institute supports major studies on the history, politics, culture, and social development of the non-Western world, with particular emphasis on the Middle East. Much of the work is interdisciplinary because of the varied interests of the Institute's fellows.

In its capacity as an institute for the advancement of peace, the Truman Research Institute initiates joint projects in both the international and local spheres, to parallel major international political activities in conflict resolution and in the struggle to uphold the principles of human rights, as defined by the UN Charter. Hence, apart from being active in academic forums, many of the Institute's members are involved in grassroots organizations.

The Truman Institute also plays an instrumental role in bringing together people from all sorts of academic and professional backgrounds, including politicians, diplomats, and journalists, to exchange ideas. This includes in-residence visiting fellows from abroad, thus reflecting the Institute's multidisciplinary and multiregional emphases. Several conferences, workshops, and symposia are organized each year. Worldwide contacts are maintained with universities, institutes, and individuals in the different fields of research. Many of the conferences, like the one held on 29 May 2008 to commemorate the fortieth anniversary of the Institute's founding, are today open to the public, thus serving to further enrich discussions and keep the work of the Truman Research Institute immediately accessible.

I wholeheartedly thank the Mandel Foundation and Ms. Barbara Mandel, our vice chairperson, for their generous support of the 2008 conference. Its program is an appropriate endeavor to help celebrate a very happy birthday to the Truman Institute for the Advancement of Peace.

INTRODUCTION

Michael J. Devine

In 1978, a conference on Hebrew University's campus in Jerusalem explored the relationship between the United States and Israel on the occasion of Israel's thirtieth anniversary. Dr. Allen Weinstein and Professor Moshe Maʿoz, participants in that event and the coeditors of the conference proceedings, stated in their preface:

> An anniversary can become either meaningful or ephemeral, depending on the amount and quality of the reflection which it inspires. This fact affects anniversary conferences such as the one which gave rise to this book. Fortunately, the occasion that brought scholars and public figures from the United States and Israel to Jerusalem in May 1978, namely a conference commemorating the thirtieth anniversary of the State of Israel, proved to be an event which provoked an intense measure of the most thoughtful commentary from all who participated.[1]

Now, thirty years after the historic 1978 conference, we are again gathered on the campus of Hebrew University to continue our exploration of the events surrounding the creation of the State of Israel and President Harry S. Truman's critical role in extending *de facto* recognition to the new state within minutes of its announced status. In 2008, we have the benefit of a vastly richer archival record, in collections held at the Truman Library and the National Archives and Records Administration in Washington, DC, as well as materials recently made available in Russia (records of the Soviet Union), Western Europe, and Israel. Thus, our program today can explore the diplomacy surrounding the establishment of Israel in greater depth and in a wider international context than was the case in 1978.

Israel's history can be seen everywhere in the National Archives and Records Administration. The history of Israel has been so intertwined with that of the

United States during the last sixty years that the National Archives now contains millions of documents, photographs, films, sound recordings, and from recent years, electronic records relating to Israel. Much of the archival record available today relating to Israel's early years was still classified in 1978.

The Truman Library, a unit of the National Archives, maintains holdings relating to Israel that amount to tens of thousands of pages, and virtually everything from Truman's administration is available to researchers. Truman's papers alone contain about 10,000 pages, including perhaps the most famous single piece of paper in the Truman Library's holdings—Truman's signed press statement announcing the United States' recognition of Israel at 6:11 p.m. Washington (DC) time, 14 May 1948.

Besides President Truman's own papers, the Truman Library has important documentation relating to Israel in the papers of Secretary of State Dean Acheson, the papers of Truman's assistant for minority affairs David K. Niles, the papers of his close friend Eddie Jacobson, and many others. Personally, I find the candid interview with George Elsey, once a young White House aide, to be particularly moving. It was recorded in 1998 and shows a sharp and still fiercely loyal assistant speaking candidly.[2] A document from Truman's papers that people always find moving is a note from Truman to Niles, dated about 12 May 1947. He is frustrated by all the politics swarming around the question of what to do with Palestine. "We could have settled this Palestine thing if U.S. politics had been kept out of it," he moans. Then he says, "I surely wish God Almighty would give the Children of Israel an Isaiah, the Christians a St. Paul and the Sons of Ishmael a peep at the golden rule."[3]

The National Archives in Washington, DC, counts its documents relating to Israel in millions. Among many other materials about Israel, it has the records of the State Department's Office of the Country Director for Israel and Arab-Israel Affairs, as well as those of the Foreign Service consulate in Jerusalem, and those of the offices that dealt with Jewish refugees and the use of the waters of the Jordan River. One can add to this the files in the records of the International Cooperation Administration that relate to U.S. aid to Israel, and the records relating to Israel in the Army Office of the Assistant Chief of Staff, G-2, Intelligence. The National Archives holds the records of the Congress too, and those contain essential Israel-related materials. I am mentioning only a few listings among hundreds of Israel-related series in the holdings of the National Archives.

In addition to these significant holdings, the National Archives' participated in the Nazi War Crimes and Japanese Imperial Government Records Interagency Working Group, which identified, declassified, and opened to the public over eight million pages in National Archives holdings relating to war crimes. Furthermore, the National Archives took the initiative about ten years ago to identify and describe about twenty million pages of documents in its holdings relating to Holocaust-era assets, including the notorious "Nazi gold."

Every presidential library[4] holds important collections relating to Israel. Modern presidents have taken much of the responsibility for developing foreign and defense policy into the White House. Therefore, the records of the National Security Council, most of which are transferred to presidential libraries when the presidents leave office, contain extremely important documentation regarding Israel. It takes time to declassify and open these documents. About six years ago, for example, the National Archives opened two important series of National Security Council files from President Nixon's papers. One included the background materials that Henry Kissinger used when he was engaged in his "shuttle diplomacy" between Egypt and Israel, and Syria and Israel. Another series included the extensive files of Middle East expert Harold Saunders relating to his work on the United Nations–sponsored peace negotiations between the 1967 and 1973 wars.

Beyond record keeping, the presidential libraries serve as educational resources and produce a wide range of educational activities for schools and extensive public programs. The presidential libraries develop exhibits, provide guided tours, conduct teacher workshops, host public forums on national and international issues, and sponsor academic conferences. Each presidential library also maintains an extensive website, making archival materials, exhibits, school activities, and public programs available to millions of users worldwide.[5] In addition, presidential libraries form partnerships with sister institutions: universities, research centers, and archives throughout the United States and abroad. The Truman Library's partnership with the Truman Research Institute for the Advancement of Peace is an outstanding example of such a relationship.

This conference is intended to build upon the foundation for scholarly inquiry set thirty years ago at this beautiful facility. While the archival materials now available worldwide enable us to understand the events of sixty years ago with greater clarity, and provide a better understanding of the international complexities that surrounded Israel's establishment as a new state, we cannot begin to imagine what the next three decades may reveal. Therefore, let us plan today to advance our scholarly analysis even further by agreeing that we must gather here again thirty years from today.

In arranging this academic endeavor, every effort was made to bring into the program a wide international participation. It is regrettable, therefore, that in spite of concerted efforts, speakers from Palestinian institutions were unable to attend.

Their cancellation at the last minute denied the program an important perspective that would have been appreciated.

The conference at Hebrew University at which the papers comprising this volume were presented was facilitated by the staff of the Harry S. Truman Research Institute for the Advancement of Peace. In particular, Naama Shpeter and Jill Twersky played key roles in the planning and implementation of the program. Professor Steven Kaplan assisted the publication process enthusiastically following his appointment as the Institute director in the spring of 2009. The president of the Nebrew University, Professor Manachem Magidor, provided vital administrative support for the conference participants. The Mandel Foundation and Robert Beren, both located in Florida, provided the financial resources for the program, and Marvin Szneler, executive director of Jewish Community Relations Bureau/ American Jewish Committee (JCRB/AJC) assisted with the complex logistical issues involved in putting together an international program. Dr. Ray Geselbracht and Dr. Randy Sowell of the Truman Library staff were sources of great assistance and solid advice throughout this endeavor. Finally, a publication project requires word processing and editorial skills, and my efforts were superbly assisted by Bonnie Neelman, assistant to the director of the Truman Library, and by Barbara Smith-Mandell, the expert copy editor at the Truman State University Press.

Notes

1. Weinstein and Ma'oz, "Preface," in *Truman and the American Commitment to Israel,* 11.
2. Benson, "View from the White House: An Interview with George M. Elsey," in *Israel and the Legacy of Harry S. Truman,* ed. Devine, Wolz, and Watson.
3. Harry S. Truman Papers, President's Secretary's Files, Subject Files, Foreign Affairs, Palestine, 1945–1947, Harry S. Truman Library.
4. There are now twelve libraries in the National Archives and Records Administration (NARA) system, and the George W. Bush Library will become the thirteenth when it opens on the Southern Methodist University campus in Dallas, Texas, in a few years.
5. For an overview of the presidential libraries and their mission, see "Presidential Libraries: Programs, Policies and the Public Interest."

Works Cited

Benson, Michael T. "The View from the White House: An Interview with George M. Elsey." In Michael J. Devine, Robert Wolz, and Robert P. Watson, eds., *Israel and the Legacy of Harry S. Truman,* 81–89. Kirksville, MO: Truman State University Press, 2008.

"Presidential Libraries: Programs, Policies and the Public Interest." Special issue, *The Public Historian* 28 (Summer 2006).

Weinstein, Allen, and Moshe Ma'oz, eds. *Truman and the American Commitment to Israel: A Thirtieth Anniversary Conference.* Jerusalem: Hebrew University/Magnes Press, 1981.

Perspectives on President Truman and Middle East History

Introduction to Session 1

William A. Brown

On behalf of the Harry S. Truman Research Institute for the Advancement of Peace, I would like to introduce this program by discussing the crucial work of the Institute and sharing some of my remembrances as one who has a long association with the Institute and with the State of Israel.

My comments on the founding and history of the Truman Research Institute for the Advancement of Peace are based on my personal conversations some years ago with a key player in the establishment of the Institute, Sam Rothberg, a philanthropist from Peoria, Illinois, and a prominent benefactor of Hebrew University. On more than one occasion, Sam said that he and a small group of the American Friends of the Hebrew University approached former president Harry Truman in 1965, in Independence, Missouri. They proposed the creation, with his support, of an institution in Jerusalem that would be dedicated to furthering the knowledge of the United States, American institutions, and U.S. history and cultures. This would benefit the Israeli public, they felt, because notwithstanding all the academic exchanges, there were still deep gaps in Israeli knowledge concerning what the United States is all about. Truman initially rejected this idea, which included the request that the institution be named for him. According to Sam, Truman said something to the effect that "A lot of people want to use my name and I get a little weary of it." However, the idea came up of an institute devoted to the study of peace, and Truman reacted positively. According to Sam, Truman said something like "I do not want to go down in history as the man who dropped the bomb," meaning, of course, the atomic bombs over Hiroshima and Nagasaki. For the public record, Truman always insisted that he had never lost a night's sleep over that decision, that he had always believed he had done the right thing in ordering those nuclear attacks. However, I think this story gives us insight into how he, or anyone who had been involved in such a big decision, would reflect back on it from time to time.

The group of American Friends enthusiastically endorsed the idea, according to Sam. However, as they gathered later on, one of the delegation members asked, "What in the world are we talking about? An institute for peace? At the height of the Cold War with the Soviet Union?" It was a unique idea at that time. But they went ahead nevertheless. By the time the Institute was ready for dedication, Truman was getting frail. It was hoped that he would come to Jerusalem and deliver an appropriate speech on the subject of peace; however, he could not do it. Instead, President Lyndon Johnson sent Solicitor General Thurgood Marshall to the Hebrew University campus of Mount Scopus, and with great ceremony the Institute was dedicated with the highest dignitaries on the Israeli side and distinguished visitors from all over the world.

The Institute had its birthing problems. Early turmoil in management and direction halted programs. However, looking back over forty years, the Institute has performed well in conducting academic research related to the issue of peace. Due to budgetary limitations and the nature of the political environment in which we work, its emphasis has been largely on the Middle East. But the Institute now has relationships in Africa, Latin America, and Asia. We have lively international exchanges going on constantly, and academicians from areas of the world that are in conflict (some in even greater conflict than here in the Middle East), as well as diplomats stationed in Israel, look to the Truman Institute for information and assistance. What a surprise it was for me, having served twice in Moscow, to find that there were delegations of Russian diplomats who came to the Truman Research Institute with enthusiasm. In my day, under the Soviet Union, that would have been unthinkable. And so it is now with China and many others, including new republics in central Asia.

It is understandable that on this occasion we are focused on the key moment of Truman's very difficult, painful confrontation in 1948 with his own secretary of state, George C. Marshall, with the Joint Chiefs of Staff, the entire Defense Department, the newly created CIA, and indeed with the whole security establishment of the United States. When the question of recognizing a Jewish state in the Middle East came before the president, all of those mentioned were unanimously against such a dramatic move for strategic reasons: oil, the security of Suez Canal, and the enormous international significance of the Arab world to the United States, especially our national leaders who were becoming aware of the profundity of the Cold War. Remember that this year is not just the sixtieth anniversary of the recognition of Israel; it is also the anniversary of the struggles in Turkey and Greece, and the Soviet invasion and occupation of Northern Iran. All of these confronted President Truman simultaneously. It is clear, as we focus on that precise moment in 1948, that Truman's decisions on partition, and ultimately his decision to recognize the State of Israel, were all made in the midst of a complex international contest.

The recognition of Israel began what became a complicated relationship between the United States and Israel. We now have many more declassified government documents on the American side, and they give us further insight into what became a roller-coaster relationship in the late 1940s. Let me give you a couple of examples. On 5 November 1948, right after the American presidential election in which Truman upset New York Governor Thomas E. Dewey, Dr. Chaim Weizmann, the president of the State of Israel, sent a very warm message to Truman, congratulating him on his victory and expounding on what it meant for Israel. The message was beautifully crafted. It reminded Truman of their discussions on other related matters, namely the conflict that emerged over the future of the Negev and Truman's pledge to honor the boundary line of the Negev against, as Chaim Weizmann put it, "the machinations of the British." Weizmann noted that the British were now arming the Arabs and in effect sending them as "a pack of assassins" to try to detach the Negev and some of the new areas from the Jewish state. There were additional references to the need for economic assistance.[1]

On 29 November, Truman sent a warm response in which he assured Weizmann of his commitment to Israel and to its integrity, including the Negev. Truman also restated his determination that a proper aid package from the Import-Export Bank would assist the development of the port of Haifa, notwithstanding opposition in the State Department.[2] This exchange of November 1948 is remarkable in its language and in the commitments on both sides. It is obvious that the Israeli side was using the entrée that Chaim Weizmann had made earlier that year when he was admitted to the White House to meet with Truman. Remarkably, there is no mention in this exchange between the two leaders of Israeli Prime Minister David Ben-Gurion, who was, after all, the real boss on the Israeli side. Clearly, the Israeli side had decided to use the Weizmann channel to Truman as an established line of communication and a vehicle by which eloquent, almost passionate, warm letters could be exchanged.

On 31 December, just one month after the gracious Truman letter to Weizmann, the first American special representative (later ambassador) to Israel, James G. McDonald, received a communication from the U.S. State Department ordering him immediately to meet with Ben-Gurion to deliver a very strong message crafted in the name of Truman. McDonald had to get in a special car with an armed escort, because Israel was then at war with her Arab neighbors and the Iraqi armed forces were already inside Israel. He had to take a circuitous route around Haifa to Tiberius to meet Ben-Gurion in the middle of the night and deliver this ultimatum. It turns out that Egyptian troops had invaded a portion of the Negev. The Israeli army, such as it was in those days, had responded by encircling them, and in so doing, Israeli forces entered into the Sinai-Egyptian territory. The British were furious at this Israeli incursion as reported from Cairo, and appealed to Washington for immediate U.S. intervention, threatening that otherwise they would have to invoke the 1936 Treaty of Defense between Britain and Egypt. In other words, Britain threatened to send troops. (In fact, five days later the British sent some aircraft over Israeli lines and the Israelis shot down several of them.) In this highly emotional, contentious time, McDonald had to go to Ben-Gurion in the middle of the night to deliver this ultimatum. The essence of the ultimatum stated: You will get out of Egyptian territory or the British may invoke the provisions of the 1936 treaty with Egypt. There could be "grave consequences." The government of the United States, which was the first to recognize you, and which has been so supportive and has "no desire to act drastically," may be compelled to "review our attitude" toward you.[3]

Ben-Gurion, who was recovering from an illness in Tiberius, had been forewarned by Israeli Foreign Minister Moshe Sharett. He received the American ambassador with dignity and said he would resolve this issue. Three hours later, McDonald was informed that orders had been given for an immediate Israeli withdrawal from Egyptian territory. That was that. Or was it? Because the conflict in the Sinai went on and on.

Six months later, McDonald had to deliver another ultimatum, again threatening a fundamental reassessment of the U.S. relationship with the provisional government of Israel (as it was then called) because of a standoff in Lausanne on the questions of refugees and boundaries, where the Israeli representative, Walter Eytan (later director general of the Israeli Foreign Ministry), was denied access for direct negotiations with the Arabs and was working through a Palestine Conciliation Committee (PCC). Eytan said, in essence, "The fundamental issue is whether the Arabs will make peace with us, and we are not going to make concessions about refugees, boundaries, and such matters unless and until we get a proper peace settlement." His attitude was characterized by the American member of the PCC, Mark Ethridge, as being so adamant and obdurate that McDonald was again sent to Ben-Gurion with an ultimatum in the name of President Truman. Ben-Gurion added, off the record, in replying to McDonald, a passionate remark: "The United States is a powerful country; Israel is a small and weak one. We can be crushed, but we will not commit suicide."[4]

I have often reflected, as a former American diplomat in Israel who went through his own share of crises in our relationship—the 1982 Israeli invasion of Lebanon, the Israeli bombing of the Iraqi nuclear reactor, and our efforts to restrain Israel from responding to Saddam Hussein's Scud attacks during the 1992 Gulf War, to name a few—on the terrible difficulties our first ambassador encountered in those circumstances.

It is known that Harry Truman occasionally vented against Jews and at times against the Israelis. The record is certainly there at the archives of the Truman Library. It is documented in Truman's recently discovered "Diary of 1947."[5] Here I would like to comment on President Truman's style and temperament. We should keep in mind that Harry Truman was quick to bridle against anybody, Jewish or non-Jewish, who challenged his position in public. As an old marine, I recall the time in 1950 when the Marine Corps leadership was, shall we say, acquiescing in moves by Congress to formalize an expanded United States Marine Corps at the beginning of the Korean War and attempting to gain equal status on the Joint Chiefs of Staff with the Army, Navy, and Air Force. A member of Congress who served with Captain Harry in World War I wrote a letter to the president asking what the commander in chief thought of all of this. Truman, unwisely, wrote a hasty reply and stuck it in the mailbox without clearing it through his staff. He wrote: "For your information the Marine Corps is the Navy's police force and as long as I'm President that is what it will remain. They have a propaganda machine that is almost equal to Stalin's."[6] The member of Congress immediately published the letter, there was a tremendous outcry, and Truman had to invite the U.S. Marine commandant to the White House and explain that, as a proud member of the U.S. Army artillery in World War I, he knew fully all the great contributions of the United States Marine Corps through its glorious history. He later wrote a letter of apology to the commandant of the Marine Corps and apologized personally to the Marine Corps League.

This was characteristic of the president. His quick temper got him in trouble on more than a few instances. You will recall that when his daughter, Margaret, gave a concert at Constitution Hall of the Daughters of the American Revolution, a music critic of the Washington Post named Paul Hume panned her presentation, saying essentially that she was a lovely young lady who has made a wonderful effort, but she just does not have the voice, the timbre, etc. The president got so angry that he wrote that critic a letter, stating "Some day I hope to meet you. When that happens you'll need a lot of beefsteak for black eyes, and perhaps a supporter below."[7] This missive also slipped past the White House staff and found its way to the *Washington Post,* where it was published, causing its author considerable embarrassment. So, he was a great man, but he had a temper, especially when he felt he was being bulldozed or pressured from any quarter, and sometimes he let his language get away from him. Moreover, he did not have a huge White House staff as is now the case, but those close to the Oval Office labored as best they could to prevent, or try to prevent, such literary outbreaks by a feisty president from leaving the West Wing.[8]

Let me conclude my remarks with a few comments about the Truman Research Institute, and remind you of its widespread connections. The basic decisions to establish connections with the Arab world were taken by courageous leaders like Moshe Ma'oz and Naomi Hazan and others, at a time when it was very difficult and certainly unusual, to extend the hand of academic fellowship to Palestinians, Jordanians, and Egyptians. Their relationships were created before my association with the Institute. After I became chairman of the board in the early 1990s, we did joint studies with Palestinian specialists and arranged for hydrologists from both Israeli and Palestinian sides to publish important studies on major issues that still get so little attention, one related to the fundamental question of water, which is an extremely complex and contentious issue and it was addressed in a courageous published volume. We have done many other successful projects with Palestinians and other Arab interlocutors on environment, economics, and trade relationships. The Institute's relationships and partnerships will be extremely useful if we can get the peace process reignited.

The papers presented in this first session by two distinguished Truman scholars of the Truman era will shed light on the events of 1948 and the legacy of President Harry S. Truman over the past sixty years. President Truman's decisions in both foreign and domestic affairs have been scrutinized by three questions of historians in the United States and abroad. With each reassessment of his presidency, Mr. Truman's status as one of the great leaders of the twentieth century seems to rise. No two scholars are better qualified to offer an analysis of this phenomenon than Drs. Allen Weinstein and Richard Kirkendall.

Notes

1. Weizmann to Truman, 5 November 1948, in U.S. Dept. of State, *Foreign Relations, 1948,* 5.2:1549–51.
2. Truman to Weizmann, in U.S. Dept. of State, *Foreign Relations, 1948,* 5.2:1633–34.
3. Lovett (Acting Secretary of State) to McDonald, 30 December 1948, in U.S. Dept. of State, *Foreign Relations, 1948,* 5.2:1704; and McDonald, *My Mission in Israel,* 117–24.
4. Acting Secretary of State to the Embassy in Israel, 28 May 1949, in U.S. Dept. of State, *Foreign Relations, 1945,* 6:1072–74; Government of Israel to the Government of the U.S., 8 June 1949, in U.S. Dept. of State, *Foreign Relations, 1949,* 1102–6; and McDonald, *My Mission in Israel,* 181–94.
5. Truman, 1947 Diary, 21 July entry, President's Secretary's Files, Harry S. Truman Papers. HSTL.

6. Truman to Rep. Gordon McDonough, 29 August 1950, in *Public Papers of the Presidents, Truman, 1950*, 618.
7. Truman to Paul Hume, 6 December 1950, quoted in McCullough, *Truman*, 829.
8. For examples of Truman's habit of venting his anger in his personal correspondence, see Poen, *Strictly Personal and Confidential*.

Works Cited

McCullough, David. *Truman*. New York: Simon and Schuster, 1992.

McDonald, James G. *My Mission in Israel*. New York: Simon and Schuster, 1967.

Poen, Monte ed. *Strictly Personal and Confidential: The Letters Harry Truman Never Mailed*. Boston: Little, Brown, 1982.

Public Papers of the Presidents of the United States, Harry S. Truman, 1950. Washington, DC: U.S. Government Printing Office, 1965.

U.S. Department of State. *Foreign Relations of the United States, 1945*. Vol. 8, *The Near East and Africa*. Washington, DC: U.S. Government Printing Office, 1969.

———. *Foreign Relations of the United States, 1948*. Vol. 5 (2 pts.), *The Near East and Africa*. Washington, DC: U.S. Government Printing Office, 1975–76.

———. *Foreign Relations of the United States, 1949*. Vol. 6, *The Near East and Africa*. Washington, DC: U.S. Government Printing Office, 1977.

The Truman Period as a Research Field

Richard S. Kirkendall

RESEARCH ON HARRY TRUMAN'S PRESIDENCY has evolved over half a century and moved through several stages. The writing has been influenced by what documents were open to scholars and also by developments in the larger world, including the Vietnam War and the Cold War. The opinions of scholars have not always been in harmony with the opinions of the American people, and historians have often clashed with one another. The subject continues to be controversial even though the Cold War, the event that dominated Harry's presidency, has ended very much the way he predicted it would. The field of Truman-period research now flourishes as never before, attracting scholars from around the world, largely because of the great importance for the world of Truman's foreign policy.

When Truman left office in 1953, most Americans regarded him as a failure. Yearning for an effective president, they considered him to be weak and indecisive. As his critics saw it, he had permitted the Communists to gain control of Eastern Europe and China and had failed to prevent and then to end the Korean War. Many critics appeared to assume that the United States could accomplish all that it desired, if only it were led by a great man; but it had the misfortune to be led—or rather misled—by Truman in a crucial period. In bidding farewell, Harry challenged this appraisal.[1]

The Truman period became a research field six years later, on May 8, 1959, Harry's seventy-fifth birthday and the day the Truman Library opened to researchers. I was in my first year as an assistant professor at the University of Missouri, having been hired to develop a graduate program that would take advantage of the research opportunities soon to be supplied by that library. I was not there on opening day, but my first doctoral student was. At first, the field did not move forward as rapidly as I had predicted it would. Restrictions on access to Truman's personal papers and the records of his foreign policy limited progress in the early years.[2] Truman research had good promoters, however, including Philip C. Brooks, the library's first director, and his staff, the Truman Library Institute, which provided financial support for conferences, grants, and fellowships, and the University of Missouri Press, which published many Truman books beginning in 1966.

During these early years, most American historians admired Truman's performance in the White House. A Harvard historian, Arthur M. Schlesinger, polled a sample of the profession and reported that they regarded the Missourian as "near great," chiefly because of his positive record in foreign affairs.[3] Shortly thereafter, a journalist, Cabell Phillips of the *New York Times*, authored a book-length study that emphasized Truman's impact on the presidency as well as his record in foreign affairs in building a case for his greatness.[4]

During the early years, young scholars interested in working on the Truman period had greater access to records on domestic politics and policies than on foreign affairs. Many of the early books originated as dissertations at the University of Missouri in Columbia. They included studies of housing policy, the desegregation of the armed forces, Missouri politics, Truman and the Eightieth Congress, Truman and liberalism, health care, and the reorganization of the executive branch.[5] One member of the group, Richard Davies, labeled it the "Missouri school of Truman scholars." The school, according to his definition, "tended to emphasize the positive accomplishments of the Truman administration" while recognizing some limitations and viewed the president "as a sincere and dedicated American who faced tremendous problems and attempted to deal with them to the best of his abilities."[6]

Before the end of the 1960s, a revisionist interpretation emerged that challenged the more positive views. The revisionists disliked the containment policy and maintained that Truman could and should have accomplished much more than he did in domestic affairs. One of the earliest and most controversial members of this group, Gar Alperovitz, argued in a 1965 publication that Truman's goal in using the atomic bomb against Japanese targets was not to defeat the Japanese but to contain the Soviet Union.[7] Another important contributor to the rise of Truman revisionism, Barton J. Bernstein, edited and contributed to an important volume in 1970 that brought together several historians of this persuasion, including Thomas G. Paterson, Lloyd Gardner, and Athan Theoharis. In this volume, they emphasized the large role of American ideology in the coming of the Cold War, and portrayed Truman and his aides as promoting the rise of McCarthyism and failing to do enough on behalf of civil rights. Drawing upon recently opened documents, they also reflected on the influence of the Vietnam War and the crisis inside the United States. To these historians, those events appeared to have sources in what Truman had done or failed to do.[8]

By the beginning of the 1970s, Truman research had become a field of stimulating controversy, and a group of contributors to the field, aided by the Truman Library Institute, came together in a book of essays that testified to this development. An earlier edition of *The Truman Period as a Research Field*, published in 1967 by the University of Missouri Press, had noted the emergence of the debate and included essays by two revisionists, Barton J. Bernstein and William Berman, and in 1974 a "reappraisal," also published by the University of Missouri Press, focused on the liveliness of the field. The book offered essays from both sides, Robert H. Ferrell and Alonzo L. Hamby speaking for the "traditional" or "liberal" point of view, and Lloyd Gardner and Harvard Sitkoff representing the revisionists. The contributors to the first edition, David McLellan, Richard Davies, and Elmer Cornwell Jr., as well as Bernstein and Berman, commented on the essays. Serving as editor, as I had for the first volume, I pointed out that "the contributors document the very active character of the field" and "demonstrate" that it "has become much more controversial." Contributors noted a division among revisionists between those who emphasized "the political and economic system—especially capitalism"—and those who focused "upon individuals—especially Truman—in efforts to explain undesirable developments."[9]

Although Truman revisionism was on the rise in the American historical profession, public opinion in the United States was moving in a quite different direction. Soon after Harry's death at the end of 1972, he became a national hero. There was much evidence of this, none more persuasive than the competition in 1976 between Gerald Ford and Jimmy Carter for recognition by the voters as the man who most closely resembled Harry Truman. President Ford had already placed Harry's bust in the Oval Office and his portrait in the Cabinet Room. The contributors to Truman's rise in public esteem included the authors of two best-selling books, published in 1973 and 1974: Margaret Truman, the former president's daughter and author of a biography of her father,[10] and Merle Miller, who wrote *Plain Speaking: An Oral Biography*. Miller pointed to the basic factor responsible for the upturn in Harry's reputation at this time. "It has been good to think about Harry Truman this spring and summer [of 1973]…the summer of Watergate," he began his book. "The memory of him has never been sharper, never brighter than it is now, a time when menacing, shadowy men are everywhere among us."[11] Presenting Truman as a man of good character, *Plain Speaking* encouraged readers to contrast him with Richard Nixon.

During these years, another point of view emerged among historians. Labeled post-revisionism, it accepted some and rejected much of the revisionist critique. John Lewis Gaddis was a leading representative.[12] Lynne Etheridge Davis was another. Dealing with one of the hottest debates in the profession of history by the mid-70s, the debate over the origins of the Cold War, Davis agreed with revisionists that the U.S. contributed to its origins, and questioned American efforts to influence developments in Eastern Europe, but she could not agree that hopes of obtaining markets and defeating the Left motivated those efforts. Instead, she maintained that the American commitment to "Atlantic Charter principles" blocked "acceptance of a Soviet sphere of influence in Eastern Europe."[13]

In the late 1970s, Robert Donovan reasserted the liberal interpretation that had prevailed in the earliest years of Truman historical writing, doing so in a two-volume book. He was a journalist, not a professional historian, but a journalist who admired the work of historians and engaged in historical research. Although endorsing some elements of revisionism, he was most impressed by the great contrast between what was expected of Harry and what he accomplished. His explanation of Truman's failures in domestic affairs stressed the difficulties in the situation, including a strong conservative coalition in Congress, and his interpretation of the man denied that he was swayed purely by political considerations and lacked commitments to liberal and humanitarian principles. Donovan stressed continuity rather than change when dealing with the switch from Roosevelt to Truman, believed the United States contributed to the outbreak of the Cold War but did not blame Truman, and saw political factors at work in the decision to use the atomic bomb but did not emphasize them or criticize Truman for the decision. His explanation for Truman's foreign policy emphasized the influence of the history of the 1930s—a determination not to repeat the mistakes made then.[14]

During the seventies, Truman scholars continued to be hampered by major restrictions on access to papers,[15] and some of the most important ones were in the Soviet Union. "The advance of research and interpretation enables us to see now that the crucial questions about Truman concerned Russia," I suggested in 1978. Those questions were: "What did the Russians hope to achieve? How powerful were they? What would they have accomplished if Truman had behaved differently?" Obviously, such questions could not be dealt with effectively until the

Soviets opened up their archives. Until then, I proposed, "overall interpretations of the Truman period will continue to rest upon untested assumptions."[16]

Late in the decade, the situation inside the U.S. began to improve at a new pace. Restrictions on Truman's personal letters, including the many he wrote to his wife, and the diary-like items he wrote to himself, began to fall away. Early on, those of us doing research in the Truman Library had sometimes asked ourselves why the Truman letters open to us told us so little, and we concluded that he did not like to write or to reveal much about himself. Now, well after Truman's death in 1972, we learned that he had actually put much of himself on paper. Two historians, Robert Ferrell and Monte Poen, the latter a member of the Missouri school, published many of these unusually rich documents, making them easily accessible,[17] and the new situation encouraged scholars to begin work on biographies of the man.

At the same time, the federal government's declassification program also enlarged opportunities for historians of the Truman period. I first encountered the results in the mid-1980s while working on an essay titled "Harry S. Truman and the Creation of the Air Force."[18] After grumbling in the past about restrictions on access, I found it quite exciting to read manuscripts that had originally been stamped Top Secret. During these years, other scholars benefited far more than I did from the change. One was Lawrence Kaplan, who carried forward his three decades of work on NATO, publishing a book on its formative years during the Truman presidency that expressed doubts that "any other approach would have yielded greater security or prosperity to the NATO allies."[19]

Kaplan rejected revisionism; so did Robert A. Pollard, author of another mid-80s book. He identified himself as post-revisionist and distinguished himself most sharply from Gabriel and Joyce Kolko. For them, the power of the capitalist system controlled the development of American foreign policy.[20] Pointing out that the Truman administration battled against all forms of commercial discrimination, British as well as Soviet, Pollard argued that this campaign brought economic benefits to the entire Western world but that the ultimate aim was political, not economic. American policy makers sought security and relied on foreign economic policy as "the main instrument of American security from 1945 to the eve of the Korean War."[21]

Donald R. McCoy, the author of *The Presidency of Harry S. Truman*, published in 1984, was another beneficiary of the improved opportunities for research on that subject. This author concluded that Truman and his administration made "the new American state system [a system developed under the pressures of Depression and war] a permanent fixture at home" and defined "its role on the world scene." They "made big government a permanent and pervasive feature of the American scene" and "the United States government an enduring and powerful presence in world affairs."[22]

Two books published in 1989 testified to how very rich the literature on Truman and the Truman period had become. One was a collection of thirteen strong essays presented at the Woodrow Wilson International Center in 1984 by thirteen scholars, and occasioned by the one hundredth anniversary of Truman's birth. The editor, Michael J. Lacey, proposed that the book indicated that scholars had moved beyond the debates between liberals and revisionists to a new appreciation of the great importance for the Truman years of the relation between the American state and American society.[23] The other book, a "Truman encyclopedia" that I developed, contained well over three hundred articles written by more than two hundred scholars and offered the full range and great diversity of scholarly opinion on the man and his times.[24]

The field's development did not end here, however. The past two decades have been years of quite spectacular developments, moved along by the great abundance of available documents and influenced by the ending of the Cold War, the large and long-lasting event that had begun during Truman's presidency.

The rich sources enabled three scholars, David McCullough, Robert Ferrell, and Alonzo Hamby, to write large biographies and publish them from 1992 to 1995. Shortly before the Cold War ended, William Pemberton had challenged his colleagues in the Missouri school and other readers in a highly critical biography,[25] but the new biographers offered friendly accounts. Ferrell maintained that Truman was "the right man for his time, an awkward era in domestic politics and a downright dangerous period in foreign relations" and he "took the measure of his responsibilities and made few errors" and "gained a rare balance of qualities that made him … one of the best choices fate could have provided … when Roosevelt passed on." His "principal accomplishment," this biographer concluded, "was to change the foreign policy of the United States from abstention to participation in the affairs of Europe and the world."[26] Hamby, a representative of the Missouri school, also gave Truman high marks, concluding that he was "magnificently right on … the two most important issues of his time: civil rights and the Soviet challenge."[27]

Of these three biographers, McCullough was most clearly influenced by the ending of the Cold War. He expressed this in his enthusiastic account of Truman's Farewell Address. In it, the departing president had predicted that the United States would win the Cold War, doing so as a consequence of its own strengths and the oppressive character—that "fatal flaw"—of the Communist regimes. "In the long run," he had assured the American people in 1953, "the strength of our free society, and our ideals, will prevail over a system that has respect for neither God nor man." "Read many years later, in the light of what happened at the end of the Cold War, it would seem utterly extraordinary in its prescience," this biographer exclaimed. "He appeared to know even the essence of what in fact would transpire, and more importantly, why."[28]

The end of the Cold War inspired two major Truman scholars, John Gaddis and Melvyn Leffler, to survey the event from beginning to end in two quite different books. Each recognized Truman as an important participant in the story. Neither blamed him for the Cold War nor credited him for the way it ended; neither praised him, as McCullough had, for predicting the outcome. Both called attention to the fact that since the collapse of the Soviet Union and its empire, scholars had obtained access to Soviet documents, reducing the size of a problem that had hampered Truman research for many years.[29]

Although dominant opinion about Truman among historians as well as amongst the general public in recent years has been quite favorable,[30] scholars, even the friendliest ones, such as McCullough,[31] continued to find flaws as well as strengths in the record. William Stueck, the leading historian of the Korean War, was one who offered a balanced account. "Although Truman's actions and oversights contributed to the outbreak of war in June 1950, his early response was largely sound, including his action to bolster American military power," Stueck began a summary of his findings. "While he erred badly in the fall of 1950 with his overly aggressive campaign to unite Korea, he did not compound his mistake by expanding the war beyond the peninsula. Rather, he successfully escalated the military buildup and continued multilateral diplomacy to strengthen the Western alliance." Then the historian concluded this masterful summary: "In other words, Truman learned from his mistakes rather than compounding them and left the United States in a strong position to compete effectively with the primary enemy, the Soviet Union."[32]

As was true much earlier, several scholars writing recently found much less to praise. They included Arnold Offner, the author of a forceful critique of Truman's whole foreign policy. "Throughout his presidency," this historian concluded, "Truman remained a parochial nationalist who lacked the leadership to move the U.S. away from conflict and toward détente. Instead, he promoted an ideology and politics of Cold War confrontation that became the modus operandi of successive administrations and the U.S. for the next two generations."[33] Writing more favorably of the foreign policy, Carol Anderson compared it with Truman's efforts on behalf of African-Americans and concluded that "in contrast to the 'caution and restraint' the Truman administration showed in dealing with the destructive forces engulfing the black community, its actions on the international stage were bold, innovative, and decisive."[34] Looking at the Truman presidency from a vantage point offered by environmental history, Karl Brooks offered a negative conclusion. "In eight postwar years, Truman and his appointees made big and small decisions about using nature, in America and across the globe, to meet human demands," he observed. "So consequential was the combined effect of his actions that we inhabit a disordered natural world today."[35]

Several powerful and well-researched books have challenged major revisionist themes. One challenge has come from Michael Hogan. In 1987, he contributed a major book on the Marshall Plan that focused on American efforts to change the European economy. A decade later, he looked at the building of a national security state inside the U.S. His theme emphasized a contest between the traditional political culture and the rising ideology of national security that emerged in the Truman period. He portrayed Truman as strong, informed, principled, and active, occupying a middle ground in the contest and helping to avoid a return to isolation or a move into a garrison state. Yet, Hogan concluded that even Truman departed too far from the traditional culture and that the nation might have paid a lower price for its victory in the Cold War.[36]

Truman's use of atomic bombs continued to be controversial. Although Alperovitz maintained his position,[37] Richard Frank challenged revisionist themes, including the argument that the real target was the Soviet Union, not Japan. Looking at decision making on both sides, the Japanese as well as the American, the author demonstrated that the Japanese hoped to avoid unconditional surrender and negotiate an end to the war more favorable to their interests. They were thus determined to inflict heavy losses on an invading force, and could have done so.[38]

In another recent book, Wilson Miscamble took issue with another revisionist theme. Employing the abundant evidence now open to researchers, he rejected the argument that Truman broke quickly with Roosevelt's policy of cooperation and negotiation with the Soviet Union. Instead, FDR's successor moved slowly to the conclusion that his predecessor's policy was unrealistic. Rather than praise Truman for patience, Miscamble suggested that the president should have turned more quickly to a new policy. For him, Truman did not rise to greatness until 1947 and the establishment of containment, a subject the historian had explored in an earlier book on George Kennan.[39]

Thus, the Truman period as a research field continues to move forward and to do so impressively. For me, participation in this story from the beginning has been enormously satisfying and stimulating. I have witnessed all of the stages and been influenced by many of the contributors. After half a century, this fascinating journey has led me to an interpretation of Harry Truman that emphasizes his quest for peace. By peace, he meant avoiding World War III. The great influences shaping his outlook were his many experiences with war and his many years as a Bible reader.[40] They persuaded him that the making and the preserving of peace must be his highest priority. The other major parts of his presidency were influenced by this, and were subordinate to it.

General readers in the U.S. now, evidence suggests, regard David McCullough's *Truman* as the best book on its subject. It has displaced Merle Miller's *Plain Speaking* at the top of their list. Like Gerald Ford and other recent presidents, George W. Bush shares the great admiration for Truman that those authors expressed. President Bush suggested as much on his May 2008 visit to Israel. Speaking at an event in Jerusalem marking the sixtieth anniversary of Israel's founding, he said: "Because Harry Truman did what was right instead of following the conventional wisdom, we can say today that America is Israel's oldest and best friend in the world."[41] This was only his latest effort to identify himself with the once widely criticized but now much admired president. In his own country, Harry Truman is now a national hero.

Notes

1. Kirkendall, "Harry's Farewell Address and the Historical Significance of the Truman Presidency," in *Harry's Farewell*. Other contributors and contributions to this volume included, in addition to those noted below, Alonzo L. Hamby, "The Politics of Democracy: Harry S. Truman and the American People" and "Harry Truman: A Biographer's Perspective II"; Robert M. Collins, "Economic Prosperity, Security, and Equality: Harry Truman's Farewell Claims and Presidential Achievements"; Richard B. Frank, "President Harry S. Truman's Farewell Address and the Atomic Bomb: The High Price of Secrecy"; Randall B. Woods, "The Truman Prophecy"; Ellen Schrecker, "'A Very Dangerous Course': Harry S. Truman and the Red Scare"; Susan M. Hartmann, "Behind the Silences: Challenges to the Gender Status Quo during the Truman Years"; Rachel Ida Buff, "Harry Truman, Immigration, and Ethnicity at an Imperial Moment"; Jeff Gall, "Using the Farewell Address to Teach the Truman Presidency"; and Robert H. Ferrell, "Harry Truman: A Biographer's Perspective I."
2. Kirkendall, "Presidential Libraries—One Researcher's Point of View"; Kirkendall, "A Second Look at Presidential Libraries"; and Geselbracht, "Creating the Harry S. Truman Library: The First Fifty Years."
3. Schlesinger, *Paths to the Present*, 105–6.
4. Phillips, *Truman Presidency*.
5. Davies, *Housing Reform during the Truman Administration;* Dorsett, *Pendergast Machine;* Mitchell, *Embattled Democracy;* Dalfiume, *Desegregation of the U.S. Armed Forces;* Hartmann, *Truman and the 80th Congress;* Hamby, *Beyond the New Deal;* Fink, *Labor's Search for Political Order;* Poen, *Harry S. Truman versus the Medical Lobby;* and Pemberton, *Bureaucratic Politics.* My own contributions to the Truman literature during these years

included "Truman's Path to Power"; four essays on Truman's appointees to the Supreme Court in Friedman and Israel, *Justices of the United States Supreme Court 1789-1969*, 2617-720; "Election of 1948" in Schlesinger, *History of American Presidential Elections*, 3097-211; "Harry Truman" in Borden, *America's Eleven Greatest Presidents*, 225-88; "Harry S. Truman: A Missouri Farmer in the Golden Age"; and *Harry Truman, Korea, and the Imperial Presidency*. In addition, I frequently reviewed other contributions to the literature.

6. Kirkendall, *Truman Period as a Research Field: A Reappraisal, 1972*.

7. Alperovitz, *Atomic Diplomacy*.

8. Bernstein, *Politics and Policies of the Truman Administration*. Viewing Truman from the perspective offered by the Vietnam War, another revisionist compared Truman unfavorably with Henry A. Wallace and suggested that the latter had been "vindicated by history." He was right and Truman was wrong, the argument ran, for the former had correctly prophesied that the latter's foreign policy would lead to disaster; Walton, *Henry Wallace, Harry Truman, and the Cold War*. See also Cochran, *Harry Truman and the Crisis Presidency*.

9. Kirkendall, *Truman Period*, 1972, quotes at 6, 7. After the conference that contributed to that book, the Truman Library Institute turned away from conferences that featured scholars and turned to ones focusing on people who had served in the Truman administration and recording their memories. On this change in focus, see my review in *Georgia Historical Quarterly* 66 (1982): 411-12. These conferences produced three interesting and useful volumes, all edited by Francis H. Heller and published by the Regents Press of Kansas: *The Korean War: A 25-Year Perspective* (1977); *The Truman White House: The Administration of the Presidency 1945-1953* (1980); and *Economics and the Truman Administration* (1981).

10. Truman, *Harry S. Truman*.

11. Miller, *Plain Speaking*, quote at 15.

12. Gaddis, *United States and the Origins of the Cold War, 1941-1947*.

13. Davis, *Cold War Begins*. For another good example of post-revisionism, see Anderson, *United States, Great Britain, and the Cold War, 1944-1947*.

14. Donovan, *Conflict and Crisis*; and Donovan, *Tumultuous Years*. Historians continued to publish important monographs. For examples, see Marcus, *Truman and the Steel Seizure Case*; and Weinstein, *Perjury*.

15. For a good example, see Haynes, *Awesome Power*.

16. Kirkendall, review of *Conflict and Crisis: The Presidency of Harry S. Truman, 1945-1948*, by Robert J. Donovan.

17. Ferrell, *Autobiography of Harry S. Truman*; Ferrell, *Off the Record*; Ferrell, *Dear Bess*; Poen, *Strictly Personal and Confidential*; and Poen, *Letters Home by Harry Truman*.

18. Kirkendall, "Harry S. Truman and the Creation of the Air Force."

19. Kaplan, *United States and NATO*. During the eighties, I moved to Iowa State University to develop a doctoral program in agricultural history and devoted most of my teaching and research to that field. I did publish several Truman items, including "Truman and the Democratic Coalition" in Weinstein and Ma'oz, *Truman and the American Commitment to Israel*; "Harry S. Truman" in Magill, *American Presidents*; *A History of Missouri*, vol. 5, *1919-1953*; and "Truman and Missouri" in *Missouri Historical Review*. I also continued to review Truman books.

20. Kolko and Kolko, *Limits of Power*.

21. Pollard, *Economic Security and the Origins of the Cold War, 1945-1950*. Some scholars during these years also looked at domestic politics and policies. Andrew J. Dunar, to cite an example, contributed *The Truman Scandals and the Politics of Morality*.

22. McCoy, *Presidency of Harry S. Truman,* quotes at 313 and 319.

23. Lacey, *Truman Presidency.*

24. Kirkendall, *Harry S. Truman Encyclopedia.*

25. Pemberton, *Harry S. Truman: Fair Dealer and Cold Warrior.*

26. Ferrell, *Harry S. Truman: A Life,* quotes at xi–xii and 246. The author or editor of more than a dozen Truman books, Ferrell's other recent titles include *Choosing Truman; The Dying President;* and *Harry S. Truman and the Cold War Revisionists.*

27. Hamby, *Man of the People,* quote at 640. Other representatives of this school also made new contributions to Truman historiography during the 1990s: Richard Davies in a biography of a Truman critic titled *Defender of the Old Guard,* and Franklin Mitchell in a study titled *Harry S. Truman and the News Media.*

28. McCullough, *Truman,* 919.

29. Gaddis, *Cold War;* and Leffler, *For the Soul of Mankind.* Gaddis's earlier contributions to Truman historiography included *Strategies of Containment* (1982), which was revised and updated in 2005 and given a somewhat different subtitle. Leffler's major contribution to Truman historiography is *A Preponderance of Power.* Gaddis also called attention to the opening of Soviet records in *We Now Know.*

30. Neal, "Putting Presidents in Their Place"; Schlesinger, "Ultimate Approval Rating"; and "C-Span Survey of Presidential Leaders," February 16, 2000, Vertical File, Truman Library.

31. See my review of McCullough: "Harry Truman as National Hero."

32. Stueck, "Truman and Korea: An Assessment of Presidential Performance," quote at 194. Stueck's reputation as a scholar of the Korean War rests chiefly on two books: *The Korean War,* and *Rethinking the Korean War.* He continues to admire an early work by David Rees titled *Korea: The Limited War.* For a look at the war from a quite different vantage point, see Cumings, *Origins of the Korean War.*

33. Offner, *Another Such Victory,* quote at 470.

34. Anderson, "Clutching at Civil Rights Straws," quote at 97. For a much larger development of her challenging argument, see her *Eyes Off the Prize.*

35. Brooks, "A Legacy in Concrete." See also Brooks, *Public Power, Private Dams.* In another recent monograph, Virgil Dean went beyond what had long been the basic study of Truman period farm politics and policy by Allen J. Matusow to argue that the Truman period was a time of "opportunity lost," of failure to develop a much-needed, long-range policy to replace the New Deal farm program. He placed some of the blame on Truman's partisanship in the 1948 campaign. See Matusow, *Farm Policies and Politics in the Truman Years;* and Dean, *An Opportunity Lost.*

36. Hogan, *The Marshall Plan;* and Hogan, *A Cross of Iron.*

37. Alperovitz, *Decision to Use the Atomic Bomb.* See also Hasegawa, *Racing the Enemy.*

38. Frank, *Downfall.* In this new era of abundant sources, still other scholars tackled the issue. Some of the best work includes Bernstein, "Understanding the Atomic Bomb and the Japanese Surrender"; and Walker, *Prompt and Utter Destruction.*

39. Miscamble, *George F. Kennan and the Making of American Foreign Policy, 1947–1950;* and Miscamble, *From Roosevelt to Truman.* Beisner's *Dean Acheson: A Life in the Cold War* is another recent and major contribution to Truman historiography. For an informed and thoughtful essay on Truman's foreign policy and the literature on it, see Heiss, "Harry S. Truman, History, and Internationalism."

40. I discuss some of this in "Faith and Foreign Policy."

41. Hunt, Associated Press, "Bush talk in Israel criticized as missed opportunity."

Works Cited

Alperovitz, Gar. *Atomic Diplomacy: Hiroshima and Potsdam; The Use of the Atomic Bomb and the American Confrontation with Soviet Power.* New York: Simon and Schuster, 1965.

———, and Sanho Tree. *The Decision to Use the Atomic Bomb and the Architecture of an American Myth.* New York: Alfred A. Knopf, 1995.

Anderson, Carol. "Clutching at Civil Rights Straws: A Reappraisal of the Truman Years and the Struggle for African American Citizenship." In Kirkendall, *Harry's Farewell,* 75–104.

———. *Eyes Off the Prize: The United Nations and the African American Struggle for Human Rights, 1944–1955.* New York: Cambridge University Press, 2003.

Anderson, Terry H. *The United States, Great Britain, and the Cold War, 1944–1947.* Columbia: University of Missouri Press, 1981.

Beisner, Robert L. *Dean Acheson: A Life in the Cold War.* New York: Oxford University Press, 2006.

Bernstein, Barton J. "Understanding the Atomic Bomb and the Japanese Surrender: Missed Opportunities, Little-Known Near Disasters, and Modern Memory." *Diplomatic History* 19 (Spring 1995): 227–73.

———, ed. *Politics and Policies of the Truman Administration.* Chicago: Quadrangle Books, 1970.

Brooks, Karl Boyd. "A Legacy in Concrete: The Truman Presidency Transforms America's Environment." In Kirkendall, *Harry's Farewell,* 299–322.

———. *Public Power, Private Dams: The Hell's Canyon High Dam Controversy.* Seattle: University of Washington Press, 2006.

Cochran, Bert. *Harry Truman and the Crisis Presidency.* New York: Funk and Wagnalls, 1973.

Cumings, Bruce. *The Origins of the Korean War.* 2 vols. Princeton: Princeton University Press, 1981, 1990.

Dalfiume, Richard M. *Desegregation of the U.S. Armed Forces: Fighting on Two Fronts, 1939–1953.* Columbia: University of Missouri Press, 1969.

Davies, Richard O. *Defender of the Old Guard: John Bricker and American Politics.* Columbus: Ohio State University Press, 1993.

———. *Housing Reform during the Truman Administration.* Columbia: University of Missouri Press, 1966.

Davis, Lynn E. *The Cold War Begins: Soviet-American Conflict over Eastern Europe.* Princeton: Princeton University Press, 1974.

Dean, Virgil. *An Opportunity Lost: The Truman Administration and the Farm Policy Debate.* Columbia: University of Missouri Press, 2006.

Donovan, Robert J. *Conflict and Crisis: The Presidency of Harry S. Truman, 1945–1948.* New York: W. W. Norton, 1977.

———. *Tumultuous Years: The Presidency of Harry S. Truman, 1949–1953.* New York: W. W. Norton, 1982.

Dorsett, Lyle W. *The Pendergast Machine.* New York: Oxford University Press, 1968.

Dunar, Andrew J. *The Truman Scandals and the Politics of Morality.* Columbia: University of Missouri Press, 1984.

Ferrell, Robert H. *Choosing Truman: The Democratic Convention of 1944.* Columbia: University of Missouri Press, 1994.

———. *The Dying President: Franklin D. Roosevelt, 1944–1945.* Columbia: University of Missouri Press, 1998.

———. *Harry S. Truman: A Life.* Columbia: University of Missouri Press, 1994.

———. *Harry S. Truman and the Cold War Revisionists.* Columbia: University of Missouri Press, 2006.

————, ed. *The Autobiography of Harry S. Truman*. Boulder: Colorado Associated University Press, 1980.

————, ed. *Dear Bess: The Letters from Harry to Bess Truman, 1910–1959*. New York: W. W. Norton, 1983.

————, ed. *Off the Record: The Private Papers of Harry S. Truman*. New York: Harper and Row, 1980.

Fink, Gary M. *Labor's Search for Political Order: The Political Behavior of the Missouri Labor Movement, 1890–1940*. Columbia: University of Missouri Press, 1974.

Frank, Richard B. *Downfall: The End of the Imperial Japanese Empire*. New York: Random House, 1999.

Friedman, Leon, and Fred L. Israel, eds. *The Justices of the United States Supreme Court 1789–1969: Their Lives and Major Opinions*. 5 vols. New York: Chelsea House/Bowker, 1969–78.

Gaddis, John Lewis. *The Cold War: A New History*. New York: Penguin Press, 2005.

————. *Strategies of Containment: A Critical Appraisal of American Postwar National Security Policy*. New York: Oxford University Press, 1982.

————. *The United States and the Origins of the Cold War, 1941–1947*. New York: Columbia University Press, 1972.

————. *We Now Know: Rethinking Cold War History*. New York: Oxford University Press, 1997.

Geselbracht, Raymond. "Creating the Harry S. Truman Library: The First Fifty Years." *The Public Historian* 28 (Summer 2006): 58.

Hamby, Alonzo L. *Beyond the New Deal: Harry S. Truman and American Liberalism*. New York: Columbia University Press, 1973.

————. *Man of the People: A Life of Harry S. Truman*. New York: Oxford University Press, 1995.

Hartmann, Susan M. *Truman and the 80th Congress*. Columbia: University of Missouri Press, 1971.

Hasegawa, Tsuyoshi. *Racing the Enemy: Stalin, Truman, and the Surrender of Japan*. Cambridge: Harvard University Press, 2005.

Haynes, Richard F. *The Awesome Power: Harry S. Truman as Commander in Chief*. Baton Rouge: Louisiana State University Press, 1973.

Heiss, Mary Ann. "Harry S. Truman, History, and Internationalism: The Farewell Address and U.S. Foreign Relations." In Kirkendall, *Harry's Farewell*, 143–72.

Heller, Francis H. *Economics and the Truman Administration*. Lawrence: Regents Press of Kansas, 1981.

————. *The Korean War: A 25-Year Perspective*. Lawrence: Regents Press of Kansas, 1977.

————. *The Truman White House: The Administration of the Presidency 1945–1953*. Lawrence: Regents Press of Kansas, 1980.

Hogan, Michael J. *A Cross of Iron: Harry S. Truman and the Origins of the National Security State*. New York: Cambridge University Press, 1998.

————. *The Marshall Plan: America, Britain, and the Reconstruction of Western Europe, 1947–1952*. New York: Cambridge University Press, 1987.

Hunt, Terence (Associated Press). "Bush talk in Israel criticized as missed opportunity: Anniversary speech fails to tackle peace process." *Seattle Post-Intelligencer*, May 15, 2008.

Kaplan, Lawrence S. *The United States and NATO: The Formative Years*. Lexington: University Press of Kentucky, 1984.

Kirkendall, Richard S. "Election of 1948." In *History of American Presidential Elections*, 4 vols., edited by Arthur M. Schlesinger Jr., 3097–211. New York: Chelsea House, 1971.

———. "Faith and Foreign Policy: An Exploration into the Mind of Harry Truman." *Missouri Historical Review* 102 (July 2008): 214–24.

———. "Harry's Farewell Address and the Historical Significance of the Truman Presidency." In Kirkendall, *Harry's Farewell*, 1–31.

———. *Harry's Farewell: Interpreting and Teaching the Truman Presidency.* Columbia: University of Missouri Press, 2004.

———. "Harry S. Truman." In *The American Presidents,* edited by Frank N. Magill, 3:626–60. Pasadena: Salem Press, 1986.

———. "Harry S. Truman: A Missouri Farmer in the Golden Age." *Agricultural History* 48 (Oct. 1974): 467–83.

———. "Harry S. Truman and the Creation of the Air Force." *Aerospace Historian* 34 (Sept. 1987): 176–84.

———. "Harry Truman." In *America's Eleven Greatest Presidents,* edited by Morton Borden, 225–88. New York: Rand McNally, 1971.

———. "Harry Truman as National Hero." Review of *Truman,* by David McCullough. *Reviews in American History* 21 (June 1993): 314–19.

———. *Harry Truman, Korea, and the Imperial Presidency.* St. Charles, MO: Forum Press, 1975.

———. *A History of Missouri.* Vol. 5, *1919–1953.* Columbia: University of Missouri Press, 1986.

———. "Presidential Libraries—One Researcher's Point of View." *American Archivist* 25 (Oct. 1962): 441–48.

———. Review of *Conflict and Crisis: The Presidency of Harry S. Truman,* by Robert J. Donovan. *The American Spectator* (March 1978): 34.

———. Review of *Economics of the Truman Administration,* edited by Francis H. Heller. *Georgia Historical Quarterly* 66 (1982): 411–12.

———. "A Second Look at Presidential Libraries." *American Archivist* 29 (July 1966): 371–86.

———. "Truman and Missouri." *Missouri Historical Review* 81 (Jan. 1987): 127–40.

———. "Truman and the Democratic Coalition." In *Truman and the American Commitment to Israel,* edited by Allen Weinstein and Moshe Ma'oz, 29–36. Jerusalem: Magnes Press, 1981.

———. "Truman's Path to Power." *Social Science* 43 (April 1968): 67–73.

———, ed. *The Harry S. Truman Encyclopedia.* Boston: G. K. Hall, 1989.

———, ed. *The Truman Period as a Research Field.* Columbia: University of Missouri Press, 1967.

———, ed. *The Truman Period as a Research Field: A Reappraisal, 1972.* Columbia: University of Missouri Press, 1974.

Kolko, Joyce, and Gabriel Kolko. *The Limits of Power: The World and United States Foreign Policy, 1945–1954.* New York: Harper and Row, 1972.

Lacey, Michael James. *The Truman Presidency.* Cambridge: Cambridge University Press, 1989.

Leffler, Melvyn P. *For the Soul of Mankind: The United States, the Soviet Union, and the Cold War.* New York: Hill and Wang, 2007.

———. *A Preponderance of Power: National Security, the Truman Administration and the Cold War.* Stanford: Stanford University Press, 1992.

Marcus, Maeva. *Truman and the Steel Seizure Case: The Limits of Presidential Power.* New York: Columbia University Press, 1977.

Matusow, Allen J. *Farm Policies and Politics in the Truman Years.* Cambridge, MA: Harvard University Press, 1967.

McCoy, Donald R. *The Presidency of Harry S. Truman.* Lawrence: University Press of Kansas, 1984.

McCullough, David. *Truman*. New York: Simon and Schuster, 1992.

Miller, Merle. *Plain Speaking*. New York: G. P. Putnam's Sons, 1974.

Miscamble, Wilson D. *From Roosevelt to Truman: Potsdam, Hiroshima, and the Cold War*. Cambridge: Cambridge University Press, 2007.

———. *George F. Kennan and the Making of American Foreign Policy, 1947–1950*. Princeton: Princeton University Press, 1992.

Mitchell, Franklin D. *Embattled Democracy: Missouri Democratic Politics, 1919–1932*. Columbia: University of Missouri Press, 1968.

———. *Harry S. Truman and the News Media: Contentious Relations, Belated Respect*. Columbia: University of Missouri Press, 1998.

Neal, Steve. "Putting Presidents in Their Place," *Chicago Sun-Times*, November 19, 1995.

Offner, Arnold A. *Another Such Victory: President Truman and the Cold War, 1945–1953*. Stanford: Stanford University Press, 2002.

Pemberton, William E. *Bureaucratic Politics: Executive Reorganization During the Truman Administration*. Columbia: University of Missouri Press, 1979.

———. *Harry S. Truman: Fair Dealer and Cold Warrior*. Boston: Twayne, 1989.

Phillips, Cabell. *The Truman Presidency: The History of a Triumphant Succession*. New York: Macmillan, 1966.

Poen, Monte M. *Harry S. Truman versus the Medical Lobby: The Genesis of Medicare*. Columbia: University of Missouri Press, 1979.

———, ed. *Letters Home by Harry Truman*. New York: G. P. Putnam's Sons, 1984.

———, ed. *Strictly Personal and Confidential: The Letters Harry Truman Never Mailed*. Boston: Little, Brown, 1982.

Pollard, Robert A. *Economic Security and the Origins of the Cold War, 1945–1950*. New York: Columbia University Press, 1985.

Rees, David. *Korea: The Limited War*. New York: St. Martin's Press, 1964.

Schlesinger, Arthur M. *Paths to the Present*. Boston: Houghton Mifflin, 1964.

Schlesinger, Arthur M., Jr. "The Ultimate Approval Rating," *New York Times Magazine*, December 15, 1996, 46–51.

Stueck, William W. *The Korean War: An International History*. Princeton: Princeton University Press, 1995.

———. *Rethinking the Korean War: A New Diplomatic and Strategic History*. Princeton: Princeton University Press, 2002.

———. "Truman and Korea: An Assessment of Presidential Performance." In Kirkendall, *Harry's Farewell*, 173–206.

Truman, Margaret. *Harry S. Truman*. New York: Morrow, 1973.

Walker, J. Samuel. *Prompt and Utter Destruction: Truman and the Use of Atomic Bombs Against Japan*. Rev. ed. Chapel Hill: University of North Carolina Press, 2004.

Walton, Richard J. *Henry Wallace, Harry Truman, and the Cold War*. New York: Viking, 1976.

Weinstein, Allen. *Perjury: The Hiss-Chambers Case*. New York: Knopf, 1978.

A Personal Reappraisal of the Man from Independence

Allen Weinstein

THIRTY YEARS AGO, WHEN ISRAEL WAS CELEBRATING its thirtieth birthday, I coedited the proceedings of a conference much like the one held in May 2008. The 1978 conference's overall theme was "Truman and the American Commitment to Israel." I also delivered a paper at the conference entitled "Presidential Reputations: Truman and the American Imagination."[1] In my essay, I described the dramatic transformation of Truman from a president held in low esteem by the American public as he left office in 1953 to one of the country's most popular and admired former chief executives by the time of the 1978 conference. One of the major factors in accounting for Truman's rise in popular esteem by 1978 was the contrast that many Americans drew between Truman (candid, honest, and speaking his own mind) and Richard Nixon (widely viewed as secretive, and driven from office for his actions during the Watergate crisis).

In the 1978 conference on the Hebrew University campus, I discussed the process by which the Man from Independence had become something of an American folk hero during the previous thirty years. I predicted that, since Truman was probably over-mythologized in 1978, he would in time be given, as I put it, "an affectionate but more realistic place in [the American] pantheon of national leaders."[2] After thirty years, this 1978 prediction has proven to be largely incorrect.

Harry Truman is still an American folk hero, maybe now more than ever. In 1978, his heroic stature was measured largely against the failed presidency of Richard Nixon and the squalor of Watergate. At that time, the American people needed (and do at this time) a hero of simple virtue and unchallenged integrity, one who spoke plainly and felt no need to delete the expletives. Harry Truman satisfied this need then and continues to satisfy it today. If president after president disappoints us, Harry Truman is still present in memory to assure us that we may hope for much more from the next person who steps forward to lead our country.

In 2008, Truman's folk hero status remains undiminished, but at least a part of my 1978 prediction is also true. Truman is being accorded an increasingly realistic place in the presidential pantheon. I did not anticipate, however, that the popular folk hero image of Truman would remain a compelling one for most Americans.

There are at least two factors responsible for this. One is the impact of additional documentation of Truman's life and career that has become available since 1978 and that reinforces the largely positive image of the man. His letters to his wife, only discovered in the 1980s after Mrs. Truman's death, many written when he could have had no thought that anyone other than Bess Truman would ever read them, depict a simple, sensitive, and candid human being. Still others of Truman's personal writings and interviews published over the past three decades have confirmed the sense of Truman as a quintessential common man with an uncommon heart and a positive outlook on life, determined to speak honestly and plainly.

Documentation in the United States, as well as new documentation from abroad, has reinforced the view that Truman was essentially correct on the larger international issues that confronted him. Even his complex role at the onset of the Cold War is increasingly viewed with understanding by historians.

Two books illustrate the fact that neither Truman as folk hero nor Truman as president is likely to decline in public esteem anytime soon. One is David McCullough's biography of Truman,[3] still the best-selling book about the president. Another seminal book, published in 2007, is Wilson Miscamble's *From Roosevelt to Truman: Potsdam, Hiroshima, and the Cold War,*[4] which won the Harry S. Truman Book Award. The book recounts Truman's attempts to understand and make policy from his revered predecessor's plans for post–World War II. The new president consulted Roosevelt's advisers and tried to do what he believed Roosevelt would have wanted. In the end, however, by the time he delivered his important "Truman Doctrine" speech in March 1947, he knew that he would have to develop his own policies to respond to a troubled global reality that Roosevelt had never anticipated. Nothing in *From Roosevelt to Truman* will detract from Truman's currently impressive reputation. In fact, Miscamble's work will only serve to enhance Truman's legacy.

So we are left for the moment with a folk hero. One very important reason for this, not yet discussed, is Truman's vision for peace in the Middle East. He recognized Israel eleven minutes after its founding, without hesitation or doubt that he was doing what had to be done, because he believed the new State of Israel would play an essential role in a peaceful Middle East.

In recent months I have been involved in an exciting new initiative led by the National Archives and Records Administration (NARA) and the Archives of Canada to enhance our documentation of the recent history of the Middle East. Whenever and wherever possible, the National Archives promotes the importance of preserving and managing significant national records—an essential element in sustaining democracy and in creating a candid account of a nation's history.

Developing archival skills and a record-keeping focus served as the major reasons for my recent trip to the Middle East, joined by Ian Wilson, librarian and archivist of Canada, and Michael Carlson, director of the Electronic and Special Media Records Services Division (NARA NWME). This trip grew out of meetings with Dr. Wilson and other members of the global records management and archival community that took place in 2007.[5] These earlier meetings focused on opening a dialogue with the Israel State Archives and the Palestine National Archives on the possibility of collaborative archival and record-keeping projects. The shared documentary heritage of the two organizations and the need for practical records management training for their staffs created a unique opportunity for both NARA and the Library and Archives of Canada to explore this proposal with our Israeli and Palestinian colleagues.

This effort was further discussed during the annual meeting last November of the International Conferences of the Round Table on Archives. The Israel State Archives, with the support of the Israeli Prime Minister's Office, invited Dr. Wilson and me to meet with its principals in Jerusalem. The head of the Palestine National Archives also agreed to a lengthy meeting with us during the visit.

What did we learn during our trip? Although the heads of the Israel State Archives and the Palestine National Archives never met, we were able to meet separately with each of them to discuss their respective archival situations and to elicit pledges of interest in cooperating with the U.S. and Canadian archivists. Then we identified collections that jointly documented aspects of the history of Israel and of the Palestinian people, such as rare and fragile Palestinian newspapers from the 1940s and selected records from the Turkish and British Mandate periods. All are eligible for digitization so that they may be accessed on the Internet in the near future.

The Israel State Archives was established in 1949, a year after the State of Israel was formed, but the Palestine National Archives has only been in existence for ten years. It was created following the establishment of the Palestinian National Authority in 1994.

A severe lack of funding and regional instability have made progress toward a truly vibrant records management and archival program difficult for the Palestinians. Training for their many records custodians is a priority for them, as is putting the archives program on a sound legislative footing.

A wider meeting of representatives, not only from Israel and the Palestinian Authority, but from other Middle East countries and Europe as well, was held in spring 2008 in Ottawa to establish an organizational structure and a steering committee for this program. This meeting also decided on strategies for funding these projects. We have already identified a number of potential federal U.S. and Canadian funding sources, as well as international sources.

My recent visit to the Middle East is part of NARA's program of international outreach. We have strengthened our relationships with the world's great democracies and enhanced our training programs to help less-developed nations improve their archival and records management practices. As democracy continues to spread around the world, the National Archives and Records Administration will continue to play a strong role in helping emerging democracies preserve and manage the vital records that contain their national histories. And nowhere is our work of greater urgency than in the Middle East.

As the legacy of President Harry S. Truman has evolved over the decades, in large part because of the availability of archival records, so too will the story of the Palestinian people in the decade following World War II develop in a much richer and more complex fabric as crucial archival materials become available to scholars.

Notes

1. Weinstein, "Presidential Reputations: Truman and the American Imagination."
2. Ibid., 47.
3. McCullough, *Truman*.
4. Miscamble, *From Roosevelt to Truman*.
5. Similar comments appeared in Weinstein, "Nurturing Archives in the Middle East."

Works Cited

McCullough, David. *Truman*. New York: Simon and Schuster, 1992.

Miscamble, Wilson D. *From Roosevelt to Truman: Potsdam, Hiroshima and the Cold War.* Cambridge: Cambridge University Press, 2007.

Weinstein, Allen. "Nurturing Archives in the Middle East." NARA *Bulletin* (Feb. 2008): 2.

———. "Presidential Reputations: Truman and the American Imagination." In *Truman and the American Commitment to Israel,* edited by Allen Weinstein and Moshe Ma'oz, 37–47. Jerusalem: Hebrew University/Magnes Press, 1981.

Israeli Statehood
and International Actors

Introduction to Session 2

Uri Bialer

Throughout the first four decades following the establishment of Israeli statehood, the creation of Israel was studied almost exclusively from a single national point of view: notably the Israeli perspective of the miraculous and heroic events of the period from 1947 to 1948, and a Palestinian review of these events culminating in their Nakbah. The last two decades have witnessed extensive global historical research, which has not only facilitated new understanding of the two viewpoints, but has shed much light on the role played by other states involved: Britain, the United States, the Soviet Union, France, Italy, and a couple of less widely known countries.

The papers presented in this section explore subjects from an international prospective. We see, for example, that far from being interested in returning to Palestine following the United Nations 1947 resolution, the British were definitely working to minimize the losses involved in their parting from Palestine. We are made aware of the agonizing gap between the Palestinian radical platform and their actual political and military abilities. Additional topics addressed in this session include an examination of the initial lack of proper military planning for war, on the Jewish side, and the complex international setting that facilitated the Israeli military's relatively rapid development from 1947 to 1948; the mechanism of policy making on the Soviet side, leading to the sensational Gromyko Declaration in May 1947, supporting the creation of two states in Palestine; and the reasons behind the March 1948 apparent withdrawal of American support of the establishment of the Jewish state.

In this section, five distinguished scholars will share their latest research on these and other topics. In doing so, they demonstrate the value of solid research in international archival resources.

Bevin, Truman, and Palestine, 1945–1948

Gabriel (Gabi) Sheffer

Introduction

IT IS WELL KNOWN THAT BRITISH-AMERICAN problematic and shifting relations concerning the Middle East in general, and Palestine in particular, began long before the establishment of the State of Israel and continued afterwards. In his memoirs, Truman himself said that the sensitive question of Palestine and America's interest in it went back to the 1917 Balfour Declaration and, of course, continued during his presidency and afterward. Due to their competing yet changing interests in the region, there were ups and downs in these British-American relationships. During certain periods the two powers agreed, while disagreement prevailed during other periods.

There is no question, however, that during and immediately following the Second World War, a number of significant clashes occurred between those two powers, which were collaborating in other matters. One of the major clashes was about the future of British control over Palestine and the fate of the Jews and Arabs there. The solution of this clash, which came in the form of the partition of Palestine and the establishment of the State of Israel, led to a new situation not only in Palestine itself but in the entire Middle East as well.

In democracies like Britain and the United States, policy and decision making are determined by relatively large groups of politicians and bureaucrats. To a great extent, the clash and the changes in the British and American governments' positions concerning Palestine were, after the end of World War II, a matter of two leading politicians—one in the United States and one in Britain.

Until World War II, the British quite effectively controlled the entire Middle

East, including Palestine. It is true that before the war, the British encountered some challenges and difficulties in their relations with the Arabs in various countries in the region (including in Palestine during the Arab uprisings of the 1920s and 1930s), and with the Jews and the Zionists. Britain also faced challenges from the main European powers, especially France, which controlled Syria and Lebanon; Italy; and Germany, which aspired to penetrate the region and replace the British and French. However, such challenges and threats were not critical for the British government. The British administrations in these countries, supported by the presence of British troops, succeeded in overcoming such difficulties and potential pressures. Therefore, it is no wonder that the region was regarded by the British themselves and by other powers as an integral and primary part of the British Empire. Most British politicians, bureaucrats, and generals strongly believed that they would be able to maintain their control over the region that had been regarded as extremely important for the empire because of its oil, its geostrategic position, and especially because it protected the passage to India through the Suez Canal.

The gradual deterioration of the British hegemonic position in the region had already begun on the eve of the Second World War and during the early stages of war itself. As a result of their growing political and military presence and interventions in various Arab countries during those early stages of the war, the Germans and the Italians seemed capable of eventually forcing the British out of the region. During those early stages of the war, the Germans' military achievements in Greece and North Africa intensified British concerns about their position in the region. In the end, of course, this scenario did not occur.

Basically, the actual challenge to the British position in the Middle East was generated by the U.S., which became involved in supporting Britain's army and was later involved in the actual fighting against the Germans and Italians in North Africa. To a lesser extent, the British were also challenged by the Soviet Union, which started showing increasing interest in the Middle East.

Even before World War II, the U.S. had some significant interests in the region such as oil, as well as some political and religious interests. For example, in 1938, due to Zionist pressures, the American administration expressed its semi-neutral position concerning Palestine. Although the U.S. was interested in the fate of the Jewish settlement in that country, it would not support the Zionists' practical demand for a national homeland.

However, against the background of the publication of the 1939 White Paper, the Americans did not approach the British government concerning the situation in Palestine. Nevertheless, the British government became concerned about the American position and the possibility of its future intervention in Palestinian affairs.

During the later stages of the war, especially after joining the fighting, the U.S.'s direct and indirect presence and involvement in Middle Eastern military, political, and economic affairs increased. Some of the principal causes, but by no means the most critical ones, that motivated the U.S. to increase its involvement in the Middle East in general, and in Palestine in particular, were the weakening of Britain; the Holocaust and its consequences; the growing tensions between Jews, Arabs, and British in Palestine; and the Jews' and Palestinian Arabs' growing demands to establish their own sovereign states in that country. For example, the Zionists' 1942 Biltmore Resolution had a certain impact on the American position vis-à-vis the Palestinian issue.

Due to the American and British apprehensions of a further possible deterioration in the situation in Palestine, and the possibility of renewed violent clashes between Jews and Arabs, which might have turned Palestine into an insoluble issue during the latter stages of the war, the two powers tried to avoid any major clashes and even to coordinate their strategy and tactics in the region in general and in Palestine in particular. One example of this coordination was the 1943 Bermuda Conference, which did not lead to any major change in the two powers' inactivity concerning saving Jews from the emerging Holocaust. In effect, despite some disagreements, mainly concerning tactics, the reasonable relations between Churchill and Roosevelt contributed to the temporary lack of evident major political clashes between the two powers concerning the situation in Palestine.

Basically, however, the British continued to formulate and nurture their strategic plans for the future of the region during the postwar period. Fundamentally, despite their weakness and vulnerable position in general, and in the Middle East in particular, the British had no intention of giving up their presence and control of either the region as a whole or of Palestine. At that stage, their principal purpose was to reorganize the entire region step by step. One of these plans was that of a Greater Syria, within which the Palestinian issue would be resolved.

Therefore, the debate in the U.S. and Britain was about each of these two powers' commitment to implement the Balfour Declaration. Unlike some of his ministers and most of the bureaucrats and military personnel involved in Middle Eastern affairs during World War II, Britain's Prime Minister Winston Churchill was, in principle, for the implementation of the Balfour Declaration, the partition of Palestine, and the establishment of a Jewish state. Churchill even successfully pressured the British cabinet to adopt such a decision. On the American side, the policy Roosevelt adopted was to leave the situation in Palestine as it was until after the war ended. Essentially, Churchill and his government followed the same tactics. During that period, the then–vice president of the U.S., Harry S. Truman, was almost not involved in this issue.

Toward the end of the war, and in view of the clashes between Jews and Arabs, the growing tension in Palestine, and the opposition to the partition plan shown by most of the military and the bureaucrats, Churchill decided to freeze the situation until the end of the war and the upcoming elections in Britain. Among other things, Churchill objected to Roosevelt's intention to meet King Ibn Saud and discuss the Palestine problem with him. Despite British opposition, Roosevelt met the king, and was extremely impressed by him and his position. Among other things, the president learned about Ibn Saud's and the Arabs' opposition to the partition of Palestine, and in principle he accepted this position. Churchill had no other choice but to meet Ibn Saud too, and to discuss his opposition to any plans to establish a Jewish state.

Before the 1945 elections in Britain, in light of the Zionists' and Arabs' growing clashes and aggressive maneuverings, for a short time Churchill decided to allow the Americans to deal with the Palestine issue. However, under pressure from his advisers, he retreated from this position.

The 1945 Crossroads

The end of the Second World War, the July 1945 elections in Britain, the Labor Party's victory in those elections, Prime Minister Clement Attlee's and Foreign Secretary Ernest Bevin's new role in shaping British policies, and the death of Roosevelt and the beginning of Truman's presidency all signaled imminent changes in the positions of the U.S. and Britain vis-à-vis the Palestine issue, the establishment of a Jewish state, the war between the Jews and Arabs in Palestine, and the partition of that country.

Unlike the allegations directed at him by Zionist and non-Zionist Jews as well as by non-Jews, Bevin, who was the leading Labor politician and who played a major role in shaping Britain's general policies after the war and until 1948, was not anti-Semitic. In the 1930s he even exhibited sympathetic attitudes towards the Jews and Zionists. After the 1945 change in Britain's government and his appointment as foreign secretary, he adopted what may be called a pro-imperial position. Accordingly, he intended to preserve Britain's position in the Middle East, including Palestine. In this context, he identified the question of Jewish immigration into Palestine and the establishment of a Jewish state there as having a major disruptive impact on the Arab states and the Palestinians, and consequently on the British position in a region that he regarded as an important part of the British Empire.

Initially, unlike Churchill's position during Roosevelt's presidency, the Attlee and Bevin government's fundamental view was that Britain alone should be in charge of any solution of the Palestine problem. They firmly supported the view that rather than partition Palestine and establish two separate states, it should become a binational state for both the Jews and Palestinians. Their idea was that such a solution would benefit Britain, which would remain in control over such a state.

The actual major change in the British government's position began as a reaction to President Truman's call for the immediate immigration of 100,000 displaced Jews to Palestine after his return from the Potsdam Conference (16 August 1945). It should be noted that because of Britain's negative position on this matter, Arab opposition, and the probable need to send American troops to support the Jewish population and control the situation in Palestine, Truman was still reluctant to strongly accept and promote the idea of a Jewish state in Palestine, an idea that by then was not strange to him.

As Bevin remarked later on various occasions, this issue of the Jewish refugees and Truman's ambiguous support of the eventual establishment of a Jewish state also triggered a modification in British-American cooperation, and introduced a most frustrating factor into the British government's position concerning imperial and colonial affairs in general, and concerning the British role in the Middle East in particular.

In any case, the British government rejected Truman's call to allow the immigration of 100,000 Jewish refugees from Europe to Palestine. However, since senior British politicians understood quite accurately that eventually Truman and the American administration would become even more closely involved in the developments in the Middle East in general, and in Palestine in particular, they tried to renew and promote the cooperation between these two powers as a significant practical tactical tool. The British invested in diplomatic attempts to reach an agreement with the U.S. about Jewish refugees and Palestine. From the conceptual strategic viewpoint, however, the Labor government rejected Truman's call to let the Jewish refugees immigrate to Palestine, and renewed its position and maneuvers concerning the cantonization of Palestine and the creation of two autonomous entities. Toward the end of 1945, the British made these positions their formal policy.

This was the general background for Bevin's initiative to establish the Anglo-American Committee of Inquiry. Bevin's aim was to persuade the Americans to cooperate with the British and work together toward reaching an international solution for the Jewish refugees as well as for the Jewish settlement in Palestine. Indeed, the establishment of this committee was announced after Attlee's visit to Washington and his talks with Truman. The committee was established and started its work in December 1945. Given the relative relaxation in tensions and reduction of clashes between the Jews and Arabs in Palestine, the Committee's tasks were to investigate the actual situation in Palestine, the possible solutions for the Palestine problem, and the immigration of Jewish refugees to Palestine.

Despite growing American interest and involvement in the Palestine question, the British position from late 1945 until mid-1946, particularly after the British government made its major strategic decision to retreat from Egypt, was that in order to maintain its position in the Middle East, Britain should not give up its presence in Palestine. The British idea was to transfer and maintain an impressive number of British troops there. Eventually, 100,000 British soldiers were stationed in Palestine.

Tensions between the Americans and British increased because of Truman's electoral needs, his pro forma pro-Zionist position, and his promotion of various demands on their behalf. Thus, when reacting to the Anglo-American Committee report (submitted on 20 April 1946), the American government insisted on implementation of the committee's recommendation to allow 100,000 Jewish refugees to legally immigrate to Palestine and the continuation of the British Mandate in that country (of course, this was a major blow to the Zionist movement and the Jews in the Yishuv—the Jewish community in Palestine).

On the other hand, in reaction to the U.S. demands, the British declared that as long as the Jews and Arabs did not stop their aggressive warlike activities and fighting, they would not proceed with implementing the committee's recommendations concerning the Jewish refugees. Because of these opposing positions concerning the committee's recommendations, tensions between the British and the U.S. intensified. The two sides then conducted talks that were intended to ease the disagreement and tension. At the same time, the British increased their military and police efforts to quell the Jewish uprising in Palestine.

Among other steps to stabilize the situation in Palestine under their firm control, the British initiated a Jewish-Arab conference in London. However, the British government clarified that regardless of the conference's outcome, they would implement Britain's own solution.

The 1946 Watershed

Given the impasse concerning the fighting targeted against the British in Palestine, many in the British government and political system began to seriously consider evacuation of that troubled country. A slow change was also occurring in the United States. Truman's uncertain position and unclear chances of being elected president in the general elections of November 1948 meant that he needed the electoral support of the Jews, especially in New York. He was also under immense internal pressure from, among others, the Zionists and their supporters in Congress to endorse the partition of Palestine and the establishment of a Jewish state.

Truman announced his support of partition on 4 October 1946, in what is known as the Yom Kippur Statement. The British, especially Bevin, who openly criticized Truman, regarded the American president as the man responsible for the fact that Britain and the U.S. were unable to forge an agreement and unable to reach a solution for the Palestine problem that the British found reasonable.

In order to influence the U.S. to reach such an agreement with them and to avoid a situation in which the U.S. would seize control over developments in Palestine—which the Americans were actually far from being enthusiastic about—Bevin and British senior politicians began to contemplate the idea that Britain would fully submit the Palestine question to the United Nations without any preconditions. Britain even warned the U.S. about this move. If implemented, it would mean that the U.S. would have to undertake full responsibility for the Palestine question, especially in light of clear signs of growing Soviet Union involvement in the region. Because of Britain's need to have American economic and political support, the main purpose of these proclamations was still to change the U.S. position and encourage Anglo-American cooperation that would lead to a binational solution. Bevin even met with Truman to persuade him to change his position, to no avail.

When the second round of the London Conference in February 1947 failed in its attempts to persuade the Jews and Arabs to accept a renewed plan for the establishment of a binational state in Palestine (on the basis of the institution of a number of autonomous cantons), and in view of the contemporaneous debate concerning the future of the British rule of India, the deterioration of the British position in the Middle East, and Britain's poor economic state, Bevin publicly declared (on 18 February 1947) Britain's transfer to the UN of responsibility for the continued rule in Palestine and the solution of the Palestine problem. Bevin's purpose was to transform the League of Nations' Mandate over Palestine into a UN trusteeship. Initially, Bevin's statement did not mean that Britain would leave Palestine, but that an attempt to win support for the idea of a binational state in Palestine should be made. In his statement, Bevin placed responsibility for this British move on the U.S.

In view of Bevin's declaration, in May 1947 the UN decided to appoint the UN Special Committee on Palestine (UNSCOP). The committee majority's principal recommendations (made on August 31, 1947) were that the British Mandate should be terminated, that Palestine should be partitioned, and that Jewish and Arab states should be established with Jerusalem under international control. This led to the UN General Assembly's decision on November 29, 1947, in favor of the partition of Palestine and the establishment of two states in that country.

In light of the British decision to evacuate India, which meant that Palestine was no longer crucial for the protection of the Suez Canal, on 20 September 1947, the British government decided to withdraw from Palestine. In the meantime, Britain's presence in Palestine had also become an economic and military burden for the British. The British decision was communicated to the UN, a step that made it irrevocable. The British government immediately set the date for the termination of the British Mandate and the transfer of power for May 15, 1948. This decision led to the establishment of Israel on that same day.

Conclusion

The following is a short assessment of Truman's role in triggering major changes in U.S. policies and their impact on the British government led by Attlee and Bevin.

It is very difficult to speculate as to what Roosevelt's position and policy vis-à-vis Palestine would have been had he not died in April 1945. Despite the changes in the Middle East in general, and in Palestine in particular, as well as the U.S.'s greater general involvement in that region, Roosevelt was inclined to cooperate and coordinate American strategic and tactical policies and actual actions with the British.

Truman was less inclined to do so regarding the Palestine problem. Thus, Truman's basic position concerning the immigration of 100,000 Jewish refugees to Palestine, the need for partition, and the establishment of a Jewish state had a tremendous impact on the British position and their moves. Truman's views and the steps he took led the British to give up the Mandate and to involve the UN in the developments in Palestine. Despite certain fluctuations in Truman's and the American government's policies in early 1948, the United States basically accepted the partition of Palestine and the creation of a Jewish state. In any event, the British evacuation and the American policy led to the establishment of the State of Israel. In his memoirs, Truman says that he was basically of the opinion that the proposed partition of Palestine could open the way for peaceful collaboration between the Arabs and Jews. He could foresee that under the proposed plan of the United Nations, the Jews and Arabs might eventually work side by side as neighbors.

In the final analysis, the combination of Britain's weaker position and the disintegration of its empire, and Truman's Yom Kippur statement, were the main factors leading to the establishment of the State of Israel despite Bevin's and the British government's opposition to such a development.

Sources

Amitzur, Ilan. *America, Britain and Palestine.* [In Hebrew.] Jerusalem: Yad Ben Zvi Publications, 1979.

Cohen, Michael Joseph. *Truman and Israel.* Berkeley: University of California Press, 1990.

Ganin, Zvi. *Truman, American Jewry and Israel, 1945–1948.* New York: Holmes and Meier, 1979.

Louis, William R. *The British Empire in the Middle East.* Oxford: Clarendon Press, 1985.

Monroe, Elizabeth. *Britain's Moment in the Middle East, 1914–1971.* London: Chatto and Windus, 1981.

Rubin, Barry M. *The Great Powers in the Middle East 1941–1947.* London: Frank Cass, 1980.

Sykes, Christopher. *Crossroads to Israel.* Cleveland: World Publishing Co., 1965.

Truman, Harry S. *Memoirs.* Vol. 1, *Year of Decisions.* New York: Doubleday, 1955.

The Arabs, Truman, and the Birth of the State of Israel

Avraham Sela

Introduction

The birth of the State of Israel was the result of distinct historical circumstances compounded by the decisions of, and interactions among, four main parties: Britain, the Mandatory power; the United States; the Zionist movement; and the Palestinian-Arabs and the Arab states. Apart from the Zionist movement and the Jewish community in Palestine, the role of President Truman, however, was the most important factor enabling the establishment of the Jewish state. Truman's impact on this process was especially significant because it was not expected by British policy makers or by the rulers of the fledgling Arab states, some of whom formally allied with Britain, or by the Palestinian-Arab leadership. In contrast, the fallout between Britain and the Zionist movement in the wake of the 1939 White Paper paved the road to a major shift in the center of international Zionist activity from Britain to the United States as a major ally.

The role of President Truman in the birth of the State of Israel must be understood against the post–World War II backdrop of new international alignments, power structures, and expectations for national independence and sovereignty among peoples hitherto ruled by foreigners. The impact of these changes was especially salient in the Middle East, whose geographical proximity to the Soviet Union and proven oil wealth rendered it a highly important strategic asset for the Western alliance in general, and for Britain, the dominant foreign power in this region, in particular. Despite this joint strategic interest, however, the Anglo-American alliance failed to forge an agreed-upon formula for handling the contradictory claims of Arabs and Zionists concerning Palestine, resulting in frustration among British policy makers and bitterness toward the Zionist impact on the American president.[1]

The existing literature on the birth of the State of Israel focuses on the diplomatic and military perspectives of the war, with particular interest in Zionist and the Allied Powers' diplomacy prior to and during the war, and hardly addresses Arab diplomacy and responses to the emerging new world order led by the United States and the Soviet Union.[2] Especially in view of the crucial role played by President Truman in the events leading to the establishment of the State of Israel, the questions are these: To what extent were the Arab leaders aware of the rapidly changing power relations on both global and regional levels? How did such awareness affect their policy making on the Palestine question? Were there missed opportunities and untried options that could have changed the course of events or tipped the political balance of the war in Palestine to their favor and if so, why were they not taken? This paper aims to explore the attitudes of the Arabs, and explain the policies they adopted towards the United States between the end of World War II and the end of the 1948 war.

Britain, the United States, and the Question of Palestine

At the end of World War II, Britain remained the dominant power in the Middle East, with sizable military forces of about 250,000 troops in Egypt and Palestine, and mutual defense treaties with Iraq, Egypt, and Transjordan, which granted Britain special military rights and in practice were meant to secure its hegemonic position in the region. In retrospect, however, the end of the war also indicated the beginning of a rapid decline of the British Empire, which was as evident in the Middle East as elsewhere in Asia and Africa, not the least because of its glaring failure to cope with the contradictory Zionist and Arab claims to Palestine.

The impact of Britain's postwar economic exhaustion on its ability to maintain its imperial commitments overseas was not immediately recognized by all British decision makers, let alone by the Arab ruling elites. The latter continued to perceive Britain as the primary power in the eastern Mediterranean for many years to come. The British policy in Palestine after the war reflected the tension between the two main approaches in Whitehall: the "little England," economic-based approach, represented by Prime Minister Attlee, and a conservative, strategically oriented approach advocating the preservation of British hegemony in the Middle East through the construction of a regional defense system, represented by Foreign Secretary Bevin and the Chiefs of Staff. Apart from the significance of the Middle East oil resources, the latter maintained that the Arab

Middle East's strategic proximity to the Soviet Union rendered it vital for the conduct of a frontline defense battle against the Soviets, hence the necessity of preserving the Suez Canal, air bases in Iraq and Transjordan, and other strategic facilities in the region in general and in Palestine in particular.[3]

Although Britain remained the dominant power in the eastern Mediterranean and Iran, due to its constrained resources it could hardly confront on its own the Soviet attempts to encroach on Turkish and Iranian sovereign territories and Soviet support for the Communist rebellion in Greece. These early manifestations of the ensuing Cold War paved the road to the Truman Doctrine, the first American foreign policy statement concerning this part of the world, which promised American support to those countries experiencing Communist and Soviet threats. The American administration's willingness to at least partly share with Britain the burden of defending Western interests in the Middle East in the face of the Soviet Union grew substantially along with the escalating Cold War and U.S. aid programs for the rehabilitation of the Western European economies, which culminated in the Marshall Plan in the summer of 1947. The success of the plan was dependent on continued flow of oil from the Middle East, especially in view of the depleted oil reserves in the United States itself, hence the shared transatlantic interest in establishing a Western-based regional defense system, despite the British decision to withdraw from India.[4]

These developments paved the road to an Anglo-American understanding on the Middle East as a primary strategic asset for these powers' interests in wartime and peacetime alike, including the acceptance of Britain as the party responsible for the organization of the region's defense. From the outset, the parties agreed to exclude the Palestine problem from the Pentagon talks beginning on 16 October 1947 in order to secure their utmost success. Despite this strategic understanding and cooperation, in the Middle East as in global affairs, the Palestine question remained a bone of contention between Great Britain and the US administration. This was mainly because of the American president's repeated personal interventions in the Palestine question, shaped primarily by domestic electoral considerations, in defiance of his administration's policy making on this matter.[5] From Whitehall's viewpoint, this was doubly frustrating because as far as the American bureaucracy—primarily the State and Defense Departments—was concerned, there was a broad agreement about the need to adopt a pro-Arab policy on Palestine as a prerequisite to securing "Arab goodwill" toward the Western powers. It was only in the fall of 1948 that Britain and U.S. foreign policies on Palestine seemed to finally come together (at least from London's viewpoint) after a long period of differences, in line with the recommendations the international mediator Folke Bernadotte submitted to the United Nations, all of which underlined the significance of this agreement for the overall relations between the two powers.[6]

The Truman Doctrine coincided with Bevin's vision of the postwar Middle East as a bulwark against Soviet and Communist penetration into the region. This objective was to be reached by establishing a regional defense system with all the regional players led by Britain and, at the same time, by providing them with substantial financial aid to boost their social and economic development, secure the stability and loyalty to Britain of the current regimes in the region and their rejection of communist ideology.[7] Practically, however, only the United States could provide such financial aid, which further underlined Britain's dependence on American cooperation in preserving its strategic position in the Middle East. Even a greater obstacle was the attitude of suspicion and mistrust with which these plans were received by the Arab nationalist elites who, with the exception of the Hashemites in Iraq and Transjordan, would accept nothing less than total independence with no commitment whatsoever to Britain's return into their court through the back door.[8]

Under these circumstances, reaching a practicable solution to the problem of Palestine epitomized Britain's declining imperial power and deadlocked position in the Middle East. By the mid-1940s, the question of Palestine had struck deep roots in the Arab and Muslim world on both public and official levels, turning it from a local Arab-Jewish conflict into an all-Arab and all-Muslim cause. Indeed, Britain's policy on Palestine during the war was carefully shaped in accordance with this reality, giving priority to regional and imperial interests at the expense of the Jewish national home. The horrific manifestations of the Holocaust and plight of Jewish survivors in Europe, however, made Britain's wartime policy on Palestine obsolete. Settling the contradictory aspirations of Zionists and Arabs in Palestine begged for a careful solution, to which Britain could not commit itself without sustaining intolerable costs to its posture in the Middle East and relations with the United States.[9]

Even before the war in Europe came to an end, the "Palestine Question" had soared high on the public agendas of the Western Allies, assuming a new urgency and international momentum, which was received with growing concern throughout the Arab world. The British Mandate in Palestine had indeed reached a dead end: on the one hand, the impact of the Holocaust on public opinion in the West manifested itself in support of the vigorous Zionist claim for a Jewish state. At the same time, the long-awaited end of the war boosted the expectations of Arab national movements in the Middle East for nothing less than full independence for all Arab lands, including Palestine. Understandably, architects of Britain's Middle East policy portrayed the Palestine question as the "focus of Britain's policy" and the "pillar of Britain's strategic interests" in the region.[10]

Though the idea of the partition of Palestine between Jews and Arabs as the ultimate solution of this problem seemed preferable among senior British policy makers, especially in the Colonial Office, the dominant viewpoint in Whitehall was that partition of Palestine would generate severe Arab violence in the region, which would destroy friendly Arab-British relations and undermine Britain's vital interests in the Middle East. These were defined in terms of communications, oil, and strategic bases, which could be preserved only by securing the "goodwill" of the Arabs. Another source of concern was the anticipated penetration of the United States and Soviet Union into the region after the war, and the implications of the Arab quest for unity on future British posture in the region.

British policy makers estimated that in view of the anticipated violent opposition of both Arabs and Jews to partition, or of Jews to a continuation of the White Paper policy, at least another division would be needed in Palestine. Such a level of reinforcement seemed unrealistic as long as the war continued, or during the year after the end of the war, due to the need to secure the occupied European territories. Even before the end of the war, Conservative Prime Minister Churchill, aware of the strong influence Jewish and Zionist organizations exercised in U.S. domestic politics, financially exhausted by the war, and dependent on American aid for Britain's own economic rehabilitation, advocated placing part of the responsibility for the Middle East—including a long-term settlement of the Palestine problem—on the American government. With the advent of a new Labor government in August 1945 led by Prime Minister Attlee, this policy was fully adopted; hence the repeated attempts of this government to win US support for a settlement in Palestine that would mitigate Zionist pressures and legitimize Britain's Palestine policy in the United States.

Although the American bureaucracy saw eye to eye with Whitehall concerning Palestine, Britain's plans for a solution to this thorny problem were repeatedly frustrated by President Truman's interference in defiance of his own government's policy planners. Hence, Britain's efforts to involve the U.S. government in forging a new long-term policy in Palestine in accordance with its strategic interests and Arab demands were undermined by the growing intervention of Truman in favor of the Zionist movement. By late 1945, the Zionist movement had made headway into the heart of America's policy making and decided to wage an armed revolt against the Mandatory government in Palestine in response to Britain's decision to maintain its policy on Jewish immigration and land sales in accordance with the 1939 White Paper. As Bevin's biographer observed, "The Jewish demands and the Arab reaction were predictable; direct intervention by the American President was not."[11]

Truman's repeated public demand, expressed shortly after taking office as the U.S. president, to let 100,000 displaced Jews enter Palestine, demonstrated utter disregard of Britain's strict limitations on Jewish immigration, in deference to Arab objections. Washington also refused to commit itself to share the military and financial burden that implementation of the recommendations of the Anglo-American Committee of Inquiry (AACI) would involve, other than in assisting the transfer of the 100,000 displaced Jews into Palestine. Even before the AACI's report was published, senior British officials had anticipated violent confrontation of British troops with both Jews and Arabs if the AACI recommendations were implemented. This led to a growing sense of weariness of, and frustration toward the Mandate, including calls to get rid of this "thankless job."[12] In view of Washington's reservations over implementation of the AACI report, many of the cabinet's members, including Prime Minister Attlee, expressed doubts about the feasibility of implementing the report, while others were calling to get rid of Britain's responsibility in Palestine. Bevin, however, remained adamant that Britain should not refer Palestine to the United Nations, arguing that implementation of the report was possible with the strategic cooperation of the United States.[13]

Truman's next unexpected act that spoiled Britain's Palestine policy was his retreat from the provincial autonomy plan, a joint Anglo-American scheme worked out in the aftermath of the AACI Report by officials from the British Foreign Office and U.S. State Department with full consent of President Truman. The plan stipulated a regime of separate "cantons" for the Jewish and Arab communities in Palestine in two separate districts in addition to the districts of Jerusalem and the Negev, which were to remain under direct British administration. The program left open the question of future development of the Jewish and Arab districts—as two independent states or as a unitary Palestinian state with a decisive Arab majority. This vagueness may explain why cantonization was acceptable to the British Foreign and Colonial Offices and initially also to the American administration, though this very unspecified future of Jewish and Arab cantons also unified the Zionists and the Arabs against it as each party feared the worst case scenario for itself.[14] Yet, despite his initial consent to cantonization, by late July Truman retreated from the provincial autonomy plan due to strong Zionist and partisan pressures with the approach of interim congressional elections scheduled for November. Nonetheless, despite the president's disappointing position, the

British government decided to go ahead and propose the program, which came to be known as the Morrison Plan, to the Jewish Agency and the Arab governments as a basis for an agreed-upon solution, and convened for this purpose the London Conference in September 1946.

Although this conference had little or no chance of success due to the unbridgeable gap between the Arab and Zionist leaderships, Bevin apparently drew support from the Zionist leaders' willingness to accept partition of Palestine as indicated by the decision made in Paris in early August, not realizing it was primarily meant to undermine the Morrison Plan, which seemed tantamount to a death sentence to the Zionist enterprise. Moreover, the "counter plan" submitted collectively by the Arab delegations at the London Conference—without consulting the Arab Higher Committee (AHC), which was not represented—unequivocally rejected any form of partition of Palestine or recognition of any collective rights for the existing Jewish community in that country. Nonetheless, Truman's statement on 4 October, in which he repeated his demand for immediate immigration of 100,000 Jews into Palestine and expressed, for the first time, support for partition of Palestine, came as a bitter surprise to the British policy makers who responded with unhidden fury.[15]

The president's statement, which was understood as support for a Jewish state, was a serious blow to Bevin's major diplomatic effort to reach an agreed-upon settlement of the Palestine question that would allow Britain to remain in Palestine for an unspecified time and to change its status as the Mandatory power. Truman's statement obviously stiffened the Zionist position against the British proposals. Despite the British gesture of releasing the Jewish leaders arrested by the Mandatory government on 29 June of that year (see below), the Zionist Congress meeting in Basel in December 1946 decided against participation in the second round of the London Conference scheduled for January 1947, boosting the hardliners' insistence on no less than an independent Jewish state, albeit in part of Palestine. The second round of the London Conference, which included unofficial talks with the Zionist leadership headed by Ben-Gurion, indeed proved to be futile. The Arab delegations—now including a Palestinian one—were utterly immovable about the British plan, insisting that Palestine should remain a unitary Arab state. Bevin's last effort of returning to the idea of a five-year binational unitary state under British trusteeship followed by independence was also rejected by the Arabs, primarily because it also stipulated continued Jewish immigration of 4,000 a month (96,000 altogether). As to the Jewish delegates, they insisted on a "viable Jewish state," which even in its narrowest borders would include a large Arab population (300,000 to 400,000) alongside some 600,000 Jews.[16]

The failure of the London Conference underlined the unbridgeable gap not only between Jews and Arabs, but also between each of the disputants and Britain itself. Indeed, it was the failure of this conference that led to Britain's decision in February 1947 to refer Palestine to the United Nations without any recommendations, to the chagrin of the American administration, assuming that the UN would decide to back up Britain's policy as represented by Bevin's plan. Indeed, as Gabriel Cohen maintained, even at this point Bevin still insisted on maintaining Britain's grip on Palestine, perceiving its reference to the United Nations as a tactical and reversible measure.[17]

After eighteen months of delays and procrastination in Britain's decision making on Palestine, the cabinet's decision to refer Palestine to the United Nations without any recommendations represented the ultimate failure of Bevin's hesitant and contradictory policies. Above all, it represented Bevin's failure to recruit the United States to a pro-Arab solution of the Palestine conflict. Bevin still hoped that the Zionist and Arab parties would be willing to make the necessary compromises that would save Britain from having to admit total failure. His wishful hopes, however, were soon to be frustrated by the Arabs, the Jews, and President Truman, whose positions remained unmoved, leading to inevitable inertia in the United Nations.

In the next few months, Britain's bargaining position on Palestine continued to weaken. Instead of extending a renewed Mandate to Britain, the unexpected support of both superpowers for a Jewish state in part of Palestine led to the appointment of the UN Special Committee on Palestine (UNSCOP) resulting in a report presenting two options: partition of Palestine into two states (the majority plan), or a unitary federative state (the minority plan). Publication of the UNSCOP report on 1 August was met with furious Arab responses on both public and official levels, leading to a growing trend on the part of the AHC and the Arab governments to prepare for armed resistance to the partition, if the UN adopted that solution.

The inevitability of this course seemed all the more likely with the 26 September 1947 statement by Secretary of the Colonies Crich Jones that his government would only execute an agreed-upon solution between the Jews and Arabs, adding that in the absence of such an agreement, Britain would relinquish the Mandate and withdraw its military and civil administration from Palestine. The statement represented Britain's last effort to pressure the U.S. administration, the Arabs, and the Jews to achieve an agreed-upon settlement that would allow Britain to preserve its position in Palestine, and thus their 26 September statement was not irreversible.[18] However, the regional and international responses to the UNSCOP report and to this statement over the next few weeks all but convinced

British policy makers and the British public that a complete withdrawal from Palestine was indeed in Britain's best interest.

The Arab States and the Question of Palestine, 1945–48

The nature of Arab responses to the reemergence of the Palestine question toward the end of the war can be explained in the context of three major trends in Arab regional and domestic politics: growing nationalization of the masses and the quest for national liberation from foreign domination; rising popular grievances in the form of social and national protest against both indigenous elites and colonial presence; and intensified rivalries among Arab rulers and competition for all-Arab leadership.

Specifically, the end of the war and consequent removal of restrictions on political activity, coupled by growing economic difficulties as a result of the withdrawal of foreign military forces from Syria, Lebanon, Iraq, and Egypt, fueled antigovernment and anti-British sentiments. Postwar conditions enabled newly emerging secular and religious, social and nationalist, radical movements to mobilize the masses for their extraparliamentary campaigns, especially in Iraq, Egypt, Syria, and Lebanon, which had undergone a rapid process of urbanization and nationalization.[19]

The growing domestic turmoil led to an increasing inclination by political elites to espouse not only an intransigent position concerning national independence but also the doctrine of pan-Arab nationalism, rendering it the dominant public discourse. Practically, political commitment to common Arab values and interests took the form of growing adoption of the Palestine issue as a core all-Arab concern and a symbol of common Arab identity. Above all, the issue of Palestine proved to be an indispensable source of legitimacy on both domestic and regional levels, which explains its rapid rise since the late 1930s to the top of the agenda of Arab ruling elites as well as of political parties and movements.

Palestine thus came to serve as a focus of regional Arab politics, stirred by interdynastic rivalries and competition for regional leadership represented by the Hashemites' ambitions of championing unity of Greater Syria (of Amir 'Abdullah of Transjordan) or the Fertile Crescent (of the Iraqi royal family) and their rivals' resistance to any change in the regional status quo, championed by the Saudi king and supported by Egypt, Yemen, Syria, and Lebanon. These rivalries often matched a web of cross-national alliances and networks of governments and political movements.

The Palestine question indeed played a unique role in enhancing *formal* common Arab action and crystallizing the regional system's nucleus, institutionalized by the foundation of the League of Arab States in March 1945. With the foundation of the League, the Arab-Palestinian national movement, still exhausted by the 1936–39 revolt and with its political leaders detained or in exile, lost any effective representation of its own cause. The question of Palestine thus became a collective Arab issue supervised by the Arab League.[20] In practice, however, the growing Arab concern over and interest in the question of Palestine, both in public opinion and at official levels, turned out to be a paralyzing influence on joint Arab action in support of the Palestinian Arab cause, diplomatically and militarily alike. This was particularly the case because of the serious blow sustained by the Palestinian Arab leadership headed by the Mufti al-Haj Amin al-Husseini, as a result of the 1936–39 Arab rebellion in Palestine and its repression by the British Mandatory power. Worse still, the Arab and international policies conducted by the Mufti prior to and during the war turned out to be disastrous for the Palestinian Arab cause once the war came to an end. In 1939 to 1941, the Mufti played a leading role in inspiring and guiding the anti-British/anti-Hashemite rebellion in Iraq led by army officers and backed by Prime Minister Rashid `Aali al-Kilani. With Britain's suppression of the short-lived rebellion, the Mufti relocated his center of activity to Nazi Germany, where he stayed until the end of the war, fostering close collaboration with the Nazi regime, serving the German war effort by helping to recruit tens of thousands of Muslims from Yugoslavia for the German army and broadcasting Nazi propaganda to the Muslims of North Africa and the Middle East. The Mufti's record of collaboration with the Nazis would render him a pariah to future British and American governments at a time when he remained a symbol of religious devotion and national heroism among the Arab-Muslim masses.[21]

The apparent success of Zionist propaganda and diplomatic efforts in the United States toward the end of the war triggered deep concern among Palestinian and Arab political leaders, followed by intensive diplomatic action on behalf of the Palestinian-Arab cause. Effectively, the Arab governments decided to extend their support to the Palestinian-Arabs in the form of three main projects: applying a boycott of the Jewish economy, "saving" Arab lands from sale to Jews, and establishing Arab propaganda offices in Washington and London to enhance public understanding of the Arab cause and check Zionist influence on public opinion.[22] In practice, the Arab governments were slow or reluctant to provide the necessary funding for any of these schemes unless it served their own narrowly defined national interests, as indicated by the Iraqi insistence on supporting the Arab propaganda offices and land-saving projects directly rather than through the collective Arab League apparatus. Specifically, the Arab governments and public media insisted that Palestine should become a unitary independent state where Jews would constitute a permanent minority, threatening that acceptance of the Zionist claims would ruin the Arabs' friendly relations with Britain and the United States.

The collective Arab rejection of the recommendations made by the Anglo-AACI indicated the growing Arab commitment to support the Arabs of Palestine "by all possible means," in addition to making an unequivocal commitment to allocate financial support to attain this purpose. In fact, given Britain's reserved position about the AACI's recommendations and reluctance to see to their implementation, the Arab governments strove to reach a consensus with Britain that would help London to retreat altogether from the Committee's recommendations rather than taking any direct action to prevent their implementation. Hence, the "extraordinary" Arab League Council meeting of prime ministers that convened in Bludan, Syria, in June 1946 rejected the option of appealing to the United Nations, giving preference to coordinating with Britain about a new policy toward Palestine. This could mean either replacing the Mandate with collective Arab trusteeship, in accordance with articles 79 to 80 of the United Nations Charter, or prolonging the British Mandate by ten years, after which Palestine would become independent.[23]

Just how polarized the Zionist and Arab positions were was demonstrated by the vigorous rejection of the AACI's recommendations throughout the Arab world. The protests, strikes, demonstrations, and militant proclamations all combined to create a sense of crisis. Apart from rejecting the immigration of 100,000 Jews into Palestine and the abolition of restrictions on land sales to Jews, the Arabs were particularly bitter about the AACI's recommendation that Palestine should become neither a Jewish nor an Arab state. The Arabs argued that with continued Jewish immigration and land purchases, a Jewish state would be inevitable.[24]

The Arab League's meeting in Bludan resulted primarily in the decision to adopt a memorandum that each member state would issue separately to Britain and the United States, phrased in a threatening tone, regarding any attempt to implement the AACI's recommendations. The threat included a hint that economic sanctions would be applied, namely an embargo on oil supplied to Britain and the United States, and that volunteers from the Arab countries would be encouraged to support the Arabs of Palestine. Indeed, similar to the Zionist position before the AACI, Arab-Palestinian leaders insisted that the Mandate should come to an end to let the Arabs decide the dispute with the Zionists on their own. Beyond declarations, however, the Arab coalition was deeply divided over policy making, making any compromise on Palestine impossible. Hence, the Iraqi pressure to adopt resolutions threatening specific economic and political sanctions against Britain and the United States if the AACI's recommendations were implemented—a position that reflected the domestic Iraqi mood concerning Palestine—was met with strong reservations by most Arab delegates, who feared that such a threat would harm their own interests. The disagreement was finally settled by accepting the Iraqi demand, albeit keeping it secret, although the resolutions on sanctions and "popular" military and financial support to the Arabs of Palestine were informally reported to the British government.[25]

As expected by most Arab delegates, the Bludan decisions and memoranda threatening to use oil sanctions against Britain and the United States made little impression on the latter's policy makers. The U.S. State and Defense Departments attempted to employ the Arab threats to urge the White House to take a pro-Arab position on Palestine despite their awareness of the unrealistic nature of the Arab threats concerning oil embargo against the Western powers. Indeed, King Ibn Sa`ud of Arabia repeatedly stated that for purely economic considerations, his oil would not be used as a political weapon. Effectively, the fact that the Bludan threat to employ oil sanctions against Britain and the United States remained secret rendered these decisions meaningless and absolutely noncommittal. Indeed, on 8 and 10 August, only two months after Bludan's decisions had been made, the governments of Jordan and Lebanon, respectively, signed agreements of concessions with the Tapline company of Aramco. A year later Syria followed suit and signed a similar agreement with this company.[26]

In contrast to the Arab intransigent position on Palestine, the Zionist movement demonstrated political realism when, at an August 1946 meeting in Paris, a decisive majority of the Jewish Agency took a historical decision to support partition and the establishment of a "viable Jewish state" in part of Palestine. The Zionist decision, which signaled a retreat from the Biltmore Program of May 1942 recommending that "Palestine be established as a Jewish Commonwealth," came in the aftermath of eight months of unified armed resistance by the three Jewish militias (Hagana, IZL, and LHI) to the British Mandate in Palestine, which peaked in mid-June 1946 with the bombing of eleven bridges connecting Palestine to the neighboring countries and the bombing a month later of the King David Hotel, where the Mandatory civil and military headquarters were located. The timing of the Paris decision reflected a sense of fear of a violent confrontation with Britain and loss of White House support, following the British comprehensive military crackdown on the Yishuv's leadership and military infrastructure on 29 June 1946 (known as Black Saturday).[27]

Above all, however, it was the Morrison plan of provincial autonomy and its perceived danger to Zionist aspirations—and yet, its potential as a basis for negotiations on partition of Palestine into two states—that determined the change in Zionist diplomacy. Contrary to the Arab collective rejection of the provincial autonomy plan even as a basis for negotiations with Britain—mainly because it was understood as laying the cornerstone to partition of Palestine and the establishment of a Jewish state—the Zionist position paved the road to secret negotiations on partition of Palestine into Jewish and Arab states with King Abdullah of Jordan and Egypt's Prime Minister Isma'il Sidqi on the one hand, and with the British government on the other. Although these negotiations resulted in no immediate tangible results, they led to an unwritten understanding between King Abdullah and the Jewish Agency on the principle of partition of Palestine between them and the establishment of a Jewish state in an unspecified part of the territory.[28]

The main opportunity the Arabs missed was Bevin's favorable position toward their claims and his willingness to impose a settlement on the Zionist party as long as Arab and American support could be secured. This was repeatedly manifested in the two rounds of the London Conference (September 1946, January 1947), which represented the dynamics of extremism dominating both domestic and inter-Arab politics. The need of Arab rulers to appease militant nationalist and Islamic groups at home ultimately led these governments to adopt uncompromising positions on Palestine, thus intensifying inter-Arab rhetorical competition. This was fairly demonstrated by the Arab Counterplan submitted in the first round of the London Conference in the absence of the AHC's representatives and without consulting with them. The plan called for the establishment of Palestine as a unified independent state with a constant Arab majority and recognition of the Jewish population as a political minority. Specifically, the plan stipulated that Jewish immigration and land sales would cease immediately and Jewish citizens would be represented in the legislature and government in accordance with their proportion—but no more than one-third—in the total population (only those residing in Palestine for at least ten years would be considered citizens, practically excluding tens of thousands of those who immigrated in the 1930s); ensured freedom of worship and protection of holy places to all religious denominations; and stated that Hebrew would be recognized officially as a second language.[29]

These relatively far-reaching compromises on the Arab part, however, proved short-lived, especially in view of Truman's statement of 4 October supporting partition of Palestine. In addition to the resentful mood this statement produced in the Arab states, the Arab governments came under bitter criticism from the AHC. In the Arab League's council session on 20 October 1946, Jamal al-Husseini argued that the Arab governments had failed to consult with the AHC's members and misrepresented the Palestinian-Arab interests. Though the Arab League's session concluded with decisions on further memoranda and protests, this criticism would have little impact. Deliberations between the AHC and the Arab League secretariat resulted in no change of the Arab Counterplan and acceptance of the AHC reservations as a noncommittal annex. The AHC insisted that Palestine should be "unitary" rather than "unified" to prevent any indication of federalism, that the proportion of Arab to Jewish representation in the legislature and government would not exceed one to six—instead of one to two according to the Arab collective plan—and citizenship for Jews would be restricted to those who lived in Palestine before 1918, effectively disenfranchising hundreds of thousands.[30] In the second round of the London Conference, now attended by the AHC—and unofficially also by the Zionist delegates—the Arab delegates, in the absence of Arab League's Secretary-General 'Azzam and other senior Arab officials, adhered to its previous principles and rejected without any discussion Bevin's plan for the establishment of a central binational government with broad autonomy for both Arab and Jewish communities and continued Jewish migration of 4,000 a month for three years. In view of the failure of the conference, the Arab delegates suggested that the Palestine question be referred to the UN, asking that Britain remain in Palestine during the interim period before Palestine became an independent state.[31]

The UN deliberations following the UNSCOP report exposed, once again, Arab rigidity and inflexibility on Palestine. The Arab delegations exhausted all possible arguments in an attempt to convince the British and U.S. governments to refrain from supporting partition, as this could lead the Arabs to vote against them in future UN resolutions. They also implicitly mentioned the Soviet Union as an alternative ally in the international organization.[32] These efforts came to an end when the U.S. and the Soviet Union announced their support for partition on 11 and 13 October, respectively. Estimating that joint American and Soviet support would ultimately lead to the approval of partition, the Arab delegations adopted another tactic aimed at convincing the American administration to withdraw or suspend its support for partition, thus preventing its approval by two-thirds of the UN members.

The main Arab effort before the decisive vote on 29 November focused on a secret effort to reach an agreement with the U.S. delegates on settling the Palestine problem on a cantonal basis, along with the principles of the provincial autonomy plan. This diplomatic effort, presented to the British and American delegates as a collective Arab position, was led by Nuri al-Sa`id, a veteran Iraqi statesman who headed his country's delegation and had a record of supporting a cantonal solution to the Palestine problem. There is no evidence, however, that these proposals, similar to ones that came also from `Azzam, were discussed at all among the Arab delegations or with the AHC's members present at the UN session. Indeed, the Arab governments tried to serve their own interests regardless of the official collective Arab position. Hence, the Jordanian minister in Cairo suggested that his country annex Palestine as a whole to its domain, enabling further Jewish immigration to Palestine, as an alternative to partition. Publicly, however, the Arab delegates remained fully committed to their counterplan at the London Conference, claiming that Palestine should be a unitary independent state.[33] In any case, the American administration refused to discuss Nuri's proposal during the UN General Assembly's deliberations. Moreover, the president's support of partition and inclusion of the Negev in the Jewish state, and the pressures exerted by the American government on China, Liberia, and Latin American countries to support partition regardless of the State Department's reservations, further frustrated the Arab hopes for blocking partition.[34]

Parallel to secret diplomacy, in the course of the official deliberations of the ad hoc committees, the Arab delegations warned their counterparts of the disastrous results of any attempt to establish a Jewish state in Palestine—bloodshed among the Jews in Palestine and the Arab countries. Following the Secretary of the Colonies' statement on 20 November that his government would not impose any settlement by force and would prevent the implementation of partition as long as the Mandate existed, the Arab delegations, concluding that implementation of partition would necessitate employment of international force, warned the Americans that this would introduce Soviet troops into the Middle East. Such forces, the Arab representatives claimed, would intensify the threat of Communist penetration in the region, which had already been in progress as a result of anticipated Jewish immigration from Eastern Europe.[35]

The Arab argument fell on fertile soil and, though it failed to change the American vote in favor of partition, its impact was seen in the next few months in the American retreat from partition. As the moment of voting on partition approached, the Arab delegations, at the instigation of the head of Pakistan's delegation, made a last desperate effort to postpone the voting by expressing their willingness to consider UNSCOP's minority proposal of a federative state. The new Arab initiative, which was made without consulting the AHC's delegate, Jamal al-Husseini, and despite Saudi Arabia's objection, was met with strong objections from the U.S. and Soviet delegations, who claimed it was a transparent effort to stall. The U.S. delegate also pointed to the absence of Jamal al-Husseini as an indication that the AHC was not party to this proposal. Indeed, Husseini later accused the Arab delegations of treason, stressing that only the Palestinian Arabs had the right to decide their fate and would not allow others to decide it.[36] The tactical nature of this "last minute" initiative notwithstanding, it could hardly have been processed at the highest international level had there not been strong advocates of the federal/cantonal idea, especially in the Iraqi, Lebanese, and Egyptian delegations.[37]

The Arab effort against the partition plan was marked by an unbridgeable gap between public and practical policies, between threats of violence and the Arab governments' real intentions regarding implementing them. The flamboyant declarations and threats of bloodshed made by Arab officials in New York and public figures in the Middle East left the impression that these were empty threats. Indeed, due to socially based interests and established dependence on the Anglo-American powers, let alone their own divisions and competition, the Arab states were by no means in a position to employ their political and economic bargaining capabilities. In fact, the Arab governments repeatedly insisted on their interest in preventing any damage to their relations with Britain and the U.S. or, alternatively, in strengthening their relations with the Soviets at the former's expense.[38]

The UN General Assembly's resolution for partition left the Arabs with one realistic choice, namely, supporting violence in Palestine to deter the international community from attempting to implement the resolution unless an international force could be deployed to undertake the mission—an option that was justly considered to be nearly impossible. This decision coincided with spontaneous Arab riots that erupted in Jerusalem immediately after the UN resolution on partition and soon expanded to other parts of the country. Facing strong public pressures at home to rush military support for the Palestinian Arabs (which radical movements nurtured for political mobilization and self-aggrandizement), the Arab governments decided to adopt a popular model whereby warfare in Palestine would be conducted by irregular volunteers from Arab countries backed by funds and arms provided by the governments. This was also the only possible option because the Arab governments could not officially operate in Palestine without violating the Mandate's sovereignty. Moreover, Britain's repeated statements that it would not allow the implementation of partition by the UN before 15 May—the date set by the British for terminating the Mandate—were interpreted by Arab leaders as signals to overturn the UN resolution.[39]

The Arab League's emergency meeting in Cairo in December 1947 indicated a deeper involvement in the Palestine question. By adopting the idea of recruiting, training, equipping, funding, and supervising irregular troops, often commanded by officers in active military service, the Arab governments moved from political to military involvement in the Palestine question. The decision reflected a joint endeavor of the Arab states and popular nationalist and Islamist movements for whom the war in Palestine provided an opportunity to promote their prestige and overshadow the government's role. The volunteers were to be mobilized from traditional communities—such as Syria's 'Alawites, Druze, and tribesmen of the Jazira, and Shi'i volunteers from south Lebanon—known for their military tradition. Yet a large segment of the volunteers came from radical opposition groups, such as the Muslim Brotherhood movement and ultranationalist activists from Iraq, Egypt, Syria, and Lebanon. These were, to a large extent, a reflection of the motives and agendas of popular heroes and cross-national political networks that had been active in anticolonial revolts since the 1920s in Syria, Iraq, Palestine, and Lebanon.[40]

The military performance of the irregular forces was by and large disappointing, if not disastrous, for the Palestinian Arabs. Despite scoring some local achievements, the fragmentation of command between the Mufti loyalists and the semiregular Army of Deliverance (Jaysh al-Inqadh), the low discipline of the latter troops and their tendency to withdraw under pressure of Jewish attacks, and occasional harassment of Palestinian Arab civilians, all contributed to the inadequacy and eventual collapse of the irregular forces once the main Jewish militia, the Hagana, opened its offensive in early April 1948. Yet though it registered few successes on the ground, the Arab military effort had a substantial impact on the U.S. government. Based on contacts with the Arab governments, by late February the State Department had pushed a plan for withdrawal from partition through a series of Security Council decisions that emphasized the inability of the UN to implement its resolution on partition peacefully, which would have paved the road for a reconsideration of the whole issue in the upcoming General Assembly session.[41]

Parallel to formulating proposals for the establishment of a trusteeship regime in Palestine, American officials endeavored to ensure Arab cooperation and support for their proposals. Yet despite the State Department's repeated requests and Arab governments' pressures on the Mufti to delegate his representative to Washington, the Palestinian-Arab leader refused to take any action before the U.S. president announced his withdrawal from partition. Once again, the Arab governments backed the Mufti's decisions while in closed diplomatic meetings with the State Department they expressed their willingness to discuss a solution on a federal-cantonal basis and to make compromises with the Jews on constitutional and immigration matters. They also stressed their willingness to remove the Mufti and other extremists from key positions in the Arab world and asked that Britain delay the end date of the Mandate until an alternative solution to partition was developed.[42]

The sense of success on the part of irregular Arab forces in Palestine, along with other factors caused the Arab leadersip to be optimistic about an American willingness to settle for something other than partition. The optimistic Arab responses to the American initiative apparently grew out of the American wish to reverse its support for partition, and successes of the irregular Arab forces in Palestine. March 1948 was the most depressing month for the Jewish population in terms of military failures and casualties, mostly resulting from attempts to maintain communication with isolated or besieged settlements, including attempts to keep the road to Jewish Jerusalem open. The Communist takeover in Czechoslovakia on 25 February served as an opportunity to remind the Americans of the significance of Arab friendship in view of the struggle between the Western and Eastern blocs, and to repeat the warning concerning penetration of Jewish Communist agents into the Middle East as immigrants to Palestine. In addition, following an American proposal, Arab governments began discussing practical arrangements for coordinated warfare against communism in the Middle East, including an exchange of information between Iraq, Egypt, Syria, and Lebanon. The intensifying Cold War also seemed to Arab governments as an opportunity to trade off their support for favorable mutual defense treaties with the Western powers.[43]

The Arab response to the official U.S. proposal to the Security Council on 19 March, by which the United States would endeavor to end hostilities, abandon the concept of partition, and recommend UN trusteeship over Palestine, was cautiously positive as the Arab states waited to see further developments. The Arab League's council, which convened in Beirut, responded by calling for disarmament of the Hagana and prevention of further Jewish immigration. While the official Arab position remained as intransigent as ever concerning partition, Arab diplomats appeared willing to cooperate with the Western powers and the UN in every possible way to establish a truce in Palestine and prevent partition, as long as the Jewish forces were disarmed.[44]

Yet the American plan was doomed to fail, not only because it was vague or because the president and the State Department held contradictory positions on it, but mainly because the administration was not willing to beef up the plan by providing military force to ensure its implementation. On 23 March, the Jewish Agency and the National Committee announced their total rejection of the trusteeship plan and any other alternative denying or postponing partition and the establishment of a Jewish state. Two days later the president, in an attempt to alter the deviation of the State Department, stated that the trusteeship regime would be temporary and that there was no retreat from partition. Yet, even without Truman's objection to the trusteeship plan, Washington was unwilling to replace British military presence in Palestine to ensure the implementation of its plan. There was also concern that an American military involvement in Palestine would have to include protecting the Jewish community against possible invasion by the Arab regular armies. In any case, the British government would not change its plans to withdraw from Palestine by 15 May and would not take part in implementing any solution that would be agreed upon by both Jews and Arabs.[45]

The American and Arab plans were further doomed by the course of military events in Palestine, which seemed increasingly the most significant factor shaping the fate of Palestine. The collapse in mid-April of the Arab irregular forces in Palestine came as a bitter surprise to the Arab governments, shifting their main concern to preventing the establishment of a Jewish state, which had become a more realistic possibility. Yet their willingness to cooperate with the American efforts to attain a truce in Palestine before 15 May were futile, and not only due to the divided Arab front and lack of control of the forces in place. The Jewish leadership was willing to accept the truce only if it would allow partition and establishment of a Jewish state, call for removal of all Arab foreign forces from Palestine, and open the gates for Jewish immigration. In contrast, the Arabs perceived the truce as a means of preventing the establishment of a Jewish state.[46]

The decision to invade Palestine with Arab regular armies and the consequent conduct of the war resulted from Arab ruling elites' deep political concern for their own security. Indeed, it was largely a preemptive measure conducted in the face of sustained popular indignation and protest in response to the Arab Palestinians' plight, particularly their mass exodus from their homes as refugees under Jewish military pressure. The decision also represented deeply disputed inter-Arab interests, which hampered the initial military effort of invasion on the night of 14/15 May, immediately at the expiration of the British Mandate. The timing of the invasion and the collective Arab statement explaining its objectives in fact indicated that the Arab governments assumed they were invading a territory without internationally acknowledged sovereignty, a fact that would exempt them from the charge of violating international law and/or the UN resolution on partition. This assumption, however, turned out to be baseless. President Truman's decision to extend *de facto* recognition to the Jewish state just a few minutes after its proclamation by the provisional government, followed shortly by recognition by the Soviet Union, became an international legal obstacle for the Arab states in their effort to nip the Jewish state in the bud, if indeed this was what they meant to accomplish. The Arab invasion and the conduct of the war, exemplified the prominence of domestic considerations in the minds of the Arab rulers, who reluctantly entered the fray against the best advice of their military echelons.[47]

Conclusion

Britain's repeated efforts to reach a reasonable solution agreed to by the two communities in dispute could not overcome the national and religious sentiments that motivated the disputants' political aspirations and mutual alienation. Bevin's calculations and efforts to secure American support for his policy in Palestine were all linked to the concept of coercion of the Jews, or at least ensuring the Arab states' acquiescence, an option that would only be realistic with full U.S. partnership and commitment.

It is in this context of Britain's ambivalent policy on the Palestine question and tendency to take a pro-Arab position that the response of the Arab ruling elites—who were largely inexperienced in the art of international relations and were counting on or following Britain's lead in this realm—to the unexpected U.S. presidential intervention in the Palestine question can be better understood. Moreover, in view of the generally pro-Arab attitude of the American State Department and diplomatic echelons in the Arab capitals, and their lack of access to the White House, Arab governments were in no position to realistically appreciate the impact of Truman's Palestine policy, let alone affect his decisions.

The Arab ruling elites, comprised of conservative notables with very narrow popular support and political legitimacy, were by and large dependent on Britain's support as a guarantee for containing the radical social and political forces of nationalists, Communists, and Islamists. Thus, in addition to the paralyzing effect of inter-Arab politics that prevented political realism in relation to the question of Palestine, Arab policy makers were further constrained by social and political challenges that disabled any possible adjustment to the new international conditions resulting from the war, especially the impact of the new and unexpected role of the U.S. president on the Palestine question.

With the benefit of hindsight, the Arab reliance on Britain concerning Palestine was not necessarily doomed to fail. The failure of Arab collective policy on Palestine, represented by the proclamation of the State of Israel, and the latter's ability to defeat the Palestinian Arabs and repel the invasion of regular Arab armies, was not primarily the result of exogenous factors—American, represented by the White House, Zionist influence in the international arena, or British constraints. Rather, it was the intransigent position advocated by the Arab Higher Committee led by the Mufti, Haj Amin al-Husseini, and publicly adopted by the Arab governments toward any solution that would include substantial Jewish immigration into Palestine and recognition of the Jews of Palestine as a political minority. The rejection of all the solutions for the conflict suggested by Britain, the United States, and the United Nations between May 1946 and November 1947—a binational unitary state, provincial autonomy, partition, or a federative state—eventually accounted for the diplomatic deadlock that rendered the use of force inevitable. The rigid, unrealistic, and ineffective Arab collective responses to these options weakened the willingness and the ability of the pro-Arab British and American decision makers to meet the essential Arab needs—namely, putting an end to continued Jewish immigration to Palestine and establishing Palestine as an independent Arab state.

Notes

1. A typical Foreign Office Arabist, Harold Beeley, stated that the growing Zionist impact on American public opinion and party politics "poisoned Britain's relations with the United States." See his "Summary on Britain's Policy and the Palestine Question, 1945–1948," attached to his letter to Burrows, 24 March 1949, PRO, FO371/75340/E4121.
2. See for example Cohen, *Palestine and the Great Powers*; Wilson, *King Abdullah, Britain and the Making of Jordan*; Shlaim, *Collusion Across the Jordan*; Pappe, *Making of the Arab-Israeli Conflict 1947–1951*; Ilan, *Origins of the Arab-Israeli Arms Race*; and Tal, *War in Palestine 1948*. For a certain exception, see Khalidi, "Arab Perspective."
3. Louis, *British Empire in the Middle East,* 104; and Bullock, *Ernest Bevin,* 113–14, 121–25. On the viewpoint of the British military command, see also Montgomery, *Memoirs of Field Marshal the Viscount Montgomery of Alamein,* 428–30.
4. Bullock, *Ernest Bevin,* 307–16, 368–70.
5. For a comprehensive study of Truman's decisions on Palestine/State of Israel, see Cohen, *Truman and Israel.*
6. Minutes by Beeley (Bevin's adviser on Palestine) and Wright (assistant director-general, Foreign Office), 8 and 11 October 1948, respectively, PRO, FO371/68379/E13309.
7. This policy was presented by Bevin in early September 1945 at a conference in London attended by all British representatives in the Middle East. For the conference's proceedings and decisions, see minutes, 6 September 1945, PRO, FO371/45379/E6954. See also Louis, *British Empire in the Middle East,* 17–22; and Bullock, *Ernest Bevin,* 114–15, 154–55.
8. Bullock, *Ernest Bevin,* 156; and Campbell to Foreign Office, Report on strong Egyptian resistance to the Anglo-American schemes of extending aid for social and economic development, 10 June 1948, PRO, FO371/68379/E8131.
9. On the development of British decision making on Palestine in the post–World War II years, see Sela, "Britain and the Palestine Question 1945–1948."
10. Grigg to Eden, 27 June 1945, PRO, FO371/45378/E4711, and 29 June 1945, PRO, FO371/45378/

E4775; and Secretary of the Colonies Hall to the cabinet, 1 September 1945, PRO, FO371/45379/E6744.

11. Bullock, *Ernest Bevin*, 48. See also Cohen, *Palestine and the Great Powers*, 50–51, 55–57.

12. Louis, *British Empire in the Middle East*, 430–33; and Bullock, *Ernest Bevin*, 298–99.

13. Discussion of the cabinet's Defense Committee, 24 April 1946, PRO, FO371/52517/E3839; and Summary of the Cabinet Office, Brook to How, 3 June 1946, PRO, FO371/52527/E5066. On Washington's approach to London's expectations, see Halifax to Bevin, 4 May 1946, PRO, FO37152521/E4098.

14. Louis, *British Empire in the Middle East*, 436–38, 454; Bullock, *Ernest Bevin*, 300; and Beeley's summary, "Britain's Policy and the Palestine Question," Beeley to Burrows, 24 March 1949, PRO, FO371/73540/E4121.

15. For the statement, see U.S. Dept. of State, *Foreign Relations, 1946*, 7:703. See also Bevin's response in the cabinet meeting, 25 October 1946, PRO, FO371/52563/E10827.

16. Cohen (*Palestine and the Great Powers*, 182–83) perceives Truman's statement and the Zionist Congress's decision as the main causes for the failure of the London Conference. For the Bevin plan, see his letter to U.S. Secretary of State, 7 February 1946, in U.S. Dept. of State, *Foreign Relations, 1946*, 5:1033–35.

17. Cohen, "Ha-Mediniyut ha-Britit," 59–60. See also Louis, *British Empire in the Middle East*, 462, 464–67; and Cohen, *Palestine and the Great Powers*, 221–22.

18. Cohen, "Ha-Mediniyut ha-Britit," 129, 134–35. See for example reports on meetings held by the High Commissioner for Palestine, Allan Cunningham, with Hussein Khalidi and Ben-Gurion, 2 October 1947, Cunningham Papers, V/1/77, Middle East Center Archive, St. Antony's College, Oxford; and Minutes by Burrows, 25 September 1947, and Foreign Office to Beirut, 7 October 1947, PRO, FO371/61882/E9665.

19. These trends are presented in Tripp, "Egypt 1945–1952." For Iraq, see a manifesto of the ultranationalist Istiqlal (Independence) Party, connecting the issue of Palestine to the freshly signed Anglo-Iraqi Treaty of Portsmouth (January 1948), in Kubba, *Mudhakkirati fi Samim al-Ahdath*, 225–27. See also Bullock, *Ernest Bevin*, 507.

20. Maddy-Weitzman, "A New Middle East?"; and Sela, *Decline of the Arab-Israeli Conflict*, 31–54.

21. On the Mufti's role and activity in Iraq, see Hirszowicz, *Third Reich and the Arab East*, 90–95, 117–20; Mattar, "Amin al-Husseini and Iraq's Quest for Independence, 4, 271–81; "The Mufti's Activity in Iraq," 1 January 1941, CZA, S/25, file 3482; and al-Sabbagh, *Fursan al-'Uruba fil-Iraq,* 109, 139, 218–20. For his activity in Germany, see Hopp, *Mufti papiere;* and Schwanitz, "Germany's Middle East Policy," 3.

22. For a comprehensive discussion of these plans and their implementation, see Sela, "Question of Palestine in the Inter-Arab System," 202–41.

23. League of Arab States, *Protocols of the Fourth Extraordinary Session,* esp. 47–48; How to Bevin, 3 July 1946, PRO, FO371/52543/E7065; and Clark to Secretary of State, 25 June 1946, in U.S. Dept. of State, *Foreign Relations, 1946,* 7:635–36.

24. See for example Stonehewer-Bird to Foreign Office, 3 May 1946, PRO, FO371/52521/E4088; Shone to Foreign Office, 5 May 1946, PRO, FO371/52521/E4136; and Tack to Secretary of State, 3 May 1946, in U.S. Dept. of State, *Foreign Relations, 1946,* 7:592–93.

25. The Arab League's Secretary-General, 'Abdullah 'Azzam, and senior Arab delegates kept the British diplomats present in Bludan updated about the proceedings and inter-Arab disagreements; see for example reports from Clayton and Smart to the Foreign Office about their talks with 'Azzam, 8 June 1946, PRO, FO371/52526/E4523; 13 June 1946, PRO, FO371/52314/E5454; and 14 June 1946, PRO, FO141/1084/384/30/46. The Bludan

Conference and decisions, including the texts of the memoranda to the British and American governments, are documented in *Report of the Parliamentary Committee of Inquiry in the Palestine Question,* 55, 58; and Iraq Government, *Taqrir Lajnat al-Tahqiq al-Niyabiyya;* League of Arab States, *Protocols of the Fourth Extraordinary Session,* esp. 101–3, 107–8.

26. Kadi, *Arab Summit Conferences and the Palestine Problem,* 83.

27. Hurewitz, *Struggle for Palestine,* 260–61; and Heller, "Me-'Hashabat ha-Shehora' la-Haluka...," 315–16.

28. Caplan and Sela, "Zionist-Egyptian Negotiations and the Partition of Palestine, 1946"; and Sela, "Maga'im Mediniyim bein Netzigei ha-Sochnut ha-Yehudit u-Memshalot 'Ever-ha Yarden u-Mitzrayim 'al Haluka, 1946."

29. Annex to minutes of Howe to Sargeant, 19 December 1946, PRO, FO371/52567/E12394; and al-Armanazi, *'Ashar Sanawat fil-Diblumasiyya,* 186–87.

30. For the text of the AHC's Memorandum presented to the London Conference, see al-Hut, *Al-Qiadat wal-Mu'assassat al-Filastiniyya,* 820–22; and *al-Wahda* (Jerusalem), December 23, 1946.

31. Protocol of the conference's last session, 13 February 1947, PRO, FO371/61748/E1386.

32. Foreign Office to UK delegation in UN, 26 September 1947, PRO, FO371/61880/E9054; and Minutes of UK delegation to UN, 24 September 1947, PRO, FO371/61530/E9225. In his memoirs, Iraqi Foreign Minister Jamali argued that the Arabs approached the Soviet Union delegation with a proposal to support them in other UN votes in return for opposing partition, which the Soviet delegation declined; al-Jamali, *Dhikrayat wa-'Ibar,* 70.

33. Cables to Foreign Office from Evans, 16 October 1947, PRO, FO371/61883/E9712; Dundas, 13 November PRO, FO371/61888/E10731; Clayton, 22 November 1947, PRO, FO371/61889/E11008; and Kirkbride, 26 November 1947, PRO, FO371/61890/E11162.

34. Beeley's minutes, 1 March 1948, PRO, FO371/68536/E3048.

35. UK delegation in the UN to Foreign Office, 25 and 27 November 1947, PRO, FO371/61890/E11127 and E11207, respectively; *al-Misri* (Egypt), 25 November 1947; Muhammad Hussein Haykal, *Mudhakkirat fil-Siyasa al-Misriyya,* 3:30; and *Report of the Parliamentary Committee of Inquiry,* 111.

36. Eilat to the Zionist Excecutive (n.d.), summarizing the Arab "last minute" activity to prevent a pro-Zionist decision by the UN, ISA, 93.03, file 2270/6. See also Jamal al-Husseini's statement on this matter, *al-Misri,* 11 February 1948.

37. Haykal, *Mudhakkirat fil-Siyasa al-Misriyya,* 35, 38–39; and Eilat, *Ha-Ma'avak 'al ha-Medina,* 458.

38. Evans to Foreign Office, 15 October 1947, PRO, FO371/61882/E9648; and "Letter from Egypt," 3 October 1947, CZA, S/25, file 9034.

39. Summary of public opinion for December 1947 based on the Lebanese press, Houston-Boswell to Attlee, 17 January 1948, PRO, FO371/68493/E1216; and Maccatti to the Foreign Secretary, 1 December 1947, in U.S. Dept. of State, *Foreign Relations, 1947,* 5:1322–26.

40. For example, the Iraqi former prime minister and general Taha al-Hashimi, Fawzi al-Qawuqji, who was appointed as the commander of the Army of Deliverance, and the Mufti, al-Haj Amin al-Husseini, and some of his followers.

41. For the development of the State Department's position, see Cooper's minutes, 21 February 1948, in U.S. Dept. of State, *Foreign Relations, 1948,* 5.2:643–45; Austin's speech in the Security Council, in ibid., 5.2:651–54; Marshall's memorandum, 5 March 1948, in ibid., 5.2:678–79; Marshall's (Top Secret) letter to Austin, 5 March 1948, in ibid., 5.2:679–81; and Eilat, *Ha-Ma'avak 'al ha-Medina,* 549–53.

42. On the Mufti's position, see al-Husri, *Mudhakkirat Taha al-Hashimi,* Pt. 2, 1942–1955, 206–7. On the AHC's position, see UK delegation to the UN to Foreign Office, 15 March 1948, PRO, FO371/68538/E3496. On the Arab delegations' position, see Cooper to Austin, 14 March 1948, in U.S. Dept. of State, *Foreign Relations, 1948,* 5.2:723–25; and *al-Misri* (Egypt), 9 and 15 March 1948. For a clear indication that U.S. State Department officials shared their intentions with the Arab representatives in the UN, see Childs to Secretary of State, 13 March 1948, in U.S. Dept. of State, *Foreign Relations, 1948,* 5.2:719; and UK delegation to the UN to Foreign Office, 13 March 1948, PRO, FO371/68538/E3431.

43. UK delegation to the UN to Foreign Office, 13 March 1948, PRO, FO371/68548/E3577; Foreign Office to Amman, 18 March 1948, PRO, FO816/27/S/885/46; Tuck to Secretary of State, 12 April 1948, National Archives (US), 890B.00/4-1248; Tuck to Secretary of State, 8 April 1948, National Archives (US), 890B.00/4-848; and British Middle East Office (Cairo) to Foreign Office, 15 April 1948, PRO, FO371/68385/E4759.

44. Maccatti to Secretary of State, 22 April 1948, in U.S. Dept. of State, *Foreign Relations, 1948,* 5.2:753; Editor's note, ibid.; Kirkbride to Foreign Office, 23 March 1948, PRO, FO371/68539/E3879; Houston-Boswell to Foreign Office, 22 March 1948, PRO, FO371/68539/E3781; *al-Misri,* 20 March 1948; and Broadmead to Foreign Office, 1 April 1948, PRO, FO371/68369/E4175.

45. Report by General Greunther to the State and Defense Departments, in U.S. Dept. of State, *Foreign Relations, 1948,* 5.2:631–33; Henderson to Marshal, 23 March 1948, in ibid., 5.2:756–57; Inverchapple to Foreign Office, 20 March 1948, PRO, FO371/67648/E3726; Bevin to Washington, 20 March 1948, PRO, FO371/68648/E3662 and E3726.

46. Minutes by Lovett on Marshall's conversation with Shertok and Epstein, 26 April 1948, in U.S. Dept. of State, *Foreign Relations, 1948,* 5.2:761–63; Eilat, *Ha-Ma'avak 'al ha-Medina,* 659; and UK delegation in the UN to Foreign Office, 1 April 1948, PRO, FO371/68540/E4173.

47. Iraq Government, *Taqrir Lajnat al-Tahqiq al-Niyabiyya; Report of the Parliamentary Committee of Inquiry in the Palestine Question,* 34, 191; and Kirkbride to Foreign Office, 1 May 1948, PRO, FO816/118/S/1014/48.

Works Cited

al-Armanazi, Najib. *'Ashar Sanawat fil-Diblumasiyya fi Samim al-Ahdath al-'Arabiyya wal-Duwaliyya.* Beirut: Dar al-Kitab al-Jadid, 1970.

al-Husri, Sati', ed. *Mudhakkirat Taha al-Hashimi,* Pt. 2, 1942–1955. Beirut: Dar al-Tali'ah, 1978.

al-Hut, Bayan Nuwayhid. *Al-Qiadat wal-Mu'assassat al-Filastiniyya, 1918–1948.* Beirut: Mu'assassat al-Dirasat al-Filastiniyya, 1981.

al-Jamali, Fadel. *Dhikrayat wa-'Ibar, karithat Filastin wa-atharuha fi al-waqi' al-'Arabi.* Beirut: Dar al-Kitab al-Jadid, 1965.

al-Sabbagh, Salah al-Din. *Fursan al-'uruba fil-Iraq.* Damascus: al-Shabab al-'Arabi, 1956.

Bullock, Allan. *Ernest Bevin, Foreign Secretary 1945–1951.* London: Heinemann, 1983.

Caplan, Neil, and Avraham Sela. "Zionist-Egyptian Negotiations and the Partition of Palestine, 1946." *Jerusalem Quarterly* 41 (Winter 1987): 19–30.

Cohen, Gabriel, "Ha-Mediniyut ha-Britit 'Erev Milhemet ha-'Atzma'ut." In *Hayeenu ke-Holmim Kovetz Mehkarim 'al Milhemet ha-Komemiyut,* edited by Yehuda Wallach, 13–178. Tel Aviv: Massada, 1985.

Cohen, Michael J. *Palestine and the Great Powers 1945–1948.* Princeton: Princeton University Press, 1982.

———. *Truman and Israel.* Berkeley: University of California Press, 1990.

Elath, Eliahu. *Ha-Ma'avak 'al ha-Medina*, vol. 2. Tel Aviv: 'Am 'Oved, 1982.

Haykal, Muhammad Hussein. *Mudhakkirat fil-Siyasa al-Misriyya,* vol. 3. Cairo: n.p., 1978.

Heller, Yossef. "Me-'Hashabat ha-Shchora' la-Haluka, Kayitz 1946 ke-Nekudat Mifne be-Toldot ha-Mediniyut ha-Tzionit." [In Hebrew.] *Zion* 43/3–4 (1981): 314–61.

Hirszowicz, Lukasz. *The Third Reich and the Arab East.* London: Routledge & K. Paul, 1966.

Hopp, Gerhard, ed. *Mufti papiere: Briefe, Memoranden, Reden und Aufrufe Amin al-Husseinis aus dem Exil, 1940–1945.* Berlin: Klaus Schwartz Verlag, 2001.

Hurewitz, J. C. *The Struggle for Palestine.* New York: Schoken, 1976.

Ilan, Amitzur. *The Origins of the Arab-Israeli Arms Race: Arms, Embargo, Military Power and Decision in the 1948 Palestine War.* New York: New York University Press, 1996.

Iraq Government. *Taqrir Lajnat al-Tahqiq al-Niyabiyya fi Qadiyyat Filastin.* Baghdad: n.p., 1949.

Kadi, Leila S. *Arab Summit Conferences and the Palestine Problem 1945–1950, 1964–1966.* Beirut: Research Center, Palestine Liberation Organization, 1966.

Khalidi, Walid. "The Arab Perspective." In *The End of the Palestine Mandate,* edited by William R. Louis and Robert W. Stookey, 104–36. Austin: University of Texas Press, 1986.

Kubba, Muhammad Mahdi. *Mudhakkirati fi Samim al-Ahdath 1918–1958.* Beirut: Dar al Tali'ah, 1963.

League of Arab States. *Protocols of the Fourth Extraordinary Session, 8.6.46–12.6.46* [In Arabic.] Cairo: n.p., 1946.

Louis, William Roger. *The British Empire in the Middle East 1945–1951.* Oxford: Clarendon Press, 1984.

Maddy-Weitzman, Bruce. "A New Middle East? The Crystallization of the Arab State System after the Second World War." In *Demise of the British Empire in the Middle East: Britain's Response to Nationalist Movements, 1943–1955,* edited by Michael J. Cohen and Martin Kolinsky, 79–92. London: Frank Cass, 1998.

Mattar, Phillip. "Amin al-Husseini and Iraq's Quest for Independence." *Arab Studies Quarterly* 6 (1984): 267–81.

Montgomery of Alemain, Bernard Law Montgomery. *The Memoirs of Field Marshal the Viscount Montgomery of Alamein.* London: Collins, 1961.

Pappe, Ilan. *The Making of the Arab-Israeli Conflict 1947–1951.* London: Tauris 1992.

Report of the Parliamentary Committee of Inquiry in the Palestine Question. [In Arabic.] Baghdad: Iraq Government, 1949.

Schwanitz, Wolfgang G. "Germany's Middle East Policy." *MERIA* 11/9 (2007). Online at http://gloria-center.org.

Sela, Avraham. "Britain and the Palestine Question 1945–1948: The Dialectic of Regional and International Constraints." In *Demise of the British Empire in the Middle East: Britain's Response to Nationalist Movements, 1943–1955,* edited by Michael J. Cohen and Martin Kolinsky, 220–46. London: Frank Cass, 1998.

———. *The Decline of the Arab-Israeli Conflict: Middle East Politics and the Search for Regional Order.* Albany: State University of New York Press, 1998.

———. "Maga'im Mediniyim bein Netzigei ha-Sochnut ha-Yehudit u-Memshalot 'Ever-ha Yarden u-Mitzrayim 'al Haluka, 1946." *Ha-Tsionut* 10 (1985): 255–78.

———. "The Question of Palestine in the Inter-Arab System, from the Foundation of the Arab League until the Invasion of Palestine by the Arab Armies 1945–1948." PhD diss., Hebrew University of Jerusalem, July 1986.

Shlaim, Avi. *Collusion Across the Jordan.* New York: Columbia University Press, 1988.

Tal, David. *War in Palestine 1948: Strategy and Diplomacy.* London: Routledge, 2004.

Tripp, Charles. "Egypt 1945–1952: The Uses of Disorder." In *Demise of the British Empire in the Middle East: Britain's Response to Nationalist Movements, 1943–1955,* edited by Michael J. Cohen and Martin Kolinsky, 112–41. London: Frank Cass, 1998.

U.S. Department of State. *Foreign Relations of the United States, 1946.* Vol. 7, *The Near East and Africa.* Washington, DC: Government Printing Office, 1969.

———. *Foreign Relations of the United States, 1947.* Vol. 5, *The Near East and Africa.* Washington, DC: U.S. Government Printing Office, 1971.

———. *Foreign Relations of the United States, 1948.* Vol. 5 (2 pts.), *The Near East and Africa.* Washington, DC: Government Printing Office, 1975–76.

Wilson, Mary C. *King Abdullah, Britain and the Making of Jordan.* Cambridge: Cambridge University Press, 1987.

Archives

CZA   Central Zionist Archive, Jerusalem, Israel
ISA   Israel State Archive, Jerusalem, Israel
        National Archives (US), Washington, DC, USA
PRO   Public Record Office, London, UK

The "Trusteeship" and the Yishuv's Military Strategy

Alon Kadish

ON 19 MARCH 1948, U.S. REPRESENTATIVE to the United Nations Security Council Warren Austin, reporting on consultations between permanent members of the Council, announced that since partition could not "at present" be peacefully implemented, the U.S. suggested a temporary trusteeship for Palestine under the responsibility of the Trustee Council of the United Nations. That council would presumably govern the country on behalf of the United Nations, and the trusteeship would continue until such time as conditions for the peaceful implementation of partition were established. The creation of such a trusteeship would first have to be adopted by the Security Council as a recommendation to the General Assembly which, in turn, would have to be convened for a special session. Austin suggested that the Security Council instruct the Palestine Commission "to suspend its efforts to implement the proposed partition plan."[1]

The new American policy was described by Abba Hillel Silver, one of the Jewish Agency's observers (with Moshe Shertok) at the Security Council, in his response to Austin's statement, as a "shocking" and "amazing reversal." "It should be clear to everyone," he argued,

> that the establishment of a trusteeship by the United Nations in Palestine will not automatically ensure peace in that country, and that force will have to be used to maintain that arrangement, just as it would have been necessary to carry out the partition decision of the United Nations.[2]

Contrary to Austin's view, the partition, Silver argued, was not an integral whole. Parts of it—such as the establishment of a Jewish state—could be implemented independently. The Jewish leadership was committed to partition. Hence, he said,

> If the United Nations Palestine Commission is unable to carry out the mandates which were assigned to it by the General Assembly, the Jewish people of Palestine will move forward in the spirit of that resolution and will do everything which is dictated by considerations of national survival and by considerations of justice and historic rights.[3]

David Ben-Gurion heard the news of the American *volte-face* on the radio. His public response, in a statement to the press issued on 20 March, was in a similar vein. Ben-Gurion declared that the new American position did not fundamentally change the situation in Palestine and did not undermine the inevitable founding of a Jewish state. This, practically speaking, would not depend on the United Nations' decision but on Jewish ability and will to bring to bear its full military potential. "We decide the fate of the country," he said. "We lay the foundation of a Jewish state and we shall erect it." Furthermore, in view of the success of the Jewish armed efforts over the past months in withstanding all Arab attacks on Jewish communities, the Jewish State "exists and will exist if we know how to defend it."[4]

Effectively, however, Ben-Gurion saw little that could be done beyond the ongoing preparations for the showdown with the Arabs, anticipated once the mandate ended and the British army left. In a meeting of the secretariat of his party, Mapai, convened on 20 March to discuss Austin's statement, at least one speaker, Haim Halperin, suggested going on the offensive.[5] Ben-Gurion answered that the Jewish community should keep to its present course, especially in matters military. The strategy should remain unchanged, that is, responsive: "We shall fight only those who fight us."[6]

Ben-Gurion's response reflected the general strategic evaluation adopted by the Yishuv's military and political leadership, based on the British stated policy of maintaining full control over the country up until the very end of the Mandate, thereby preserving the territorial status quo between Arabs and Jews. Hence, a military decision in the fight against Palestine's Arabs could only be forced after the Mandate ended and the British Army withdrew. Until then, the best that could be done was to hold on to existing assets and build up the military force necessary for the eventual decisive confrontation over the realization of the partition. The same evaluation was expressed in the preamble of Plan Dalet [D], drawn up by the Hagana High Command's Operations Branch and issued in March 1948.[7] The plan dealt with "the day after" and assumed, at the outset, that it would be put into operation when the British government's forces would not be in the country,[8] or at most remain in only a few bases and areas.[9] Once British forces withdrew, the Jewish army would face an invasion of Arab regular armies supported by semi-regular volunteers and local Arab forces. Not only was the crucial date nearly two months away, it was widely felt, not least by Yigael Yadin and other senior commanders of the Hagana, that the Jewish forces were not yet ready for war.[10] Israel Galilee's (a leader of the Hagana) view was that the best Jewish course was to bide their time and avoid confrontations.

Nevertheless, a strategic change did occur, due not to a change in Jewish strategic thinking, but to a series of redeployments of British forces that enabled both sides to initiate local offensives. These gradually and accumulatively constituted a strategic change, whereby the Jews had effectively beaten the Palestinian Arabs by the time the Mandate had ended and before the regular Arab armies could invade Palestine.

From the outset of the hostilities in Palestine, after the United Nations adopted the Partition Resolution, the British army found itself in an increasingly difficult situation. The army had been in the process of continuous contraction, with units being amalgamated or shut down altogether. As the intercommunity violence escalated in Palestine, fewer and fewer troops were available to deal with an increasing number of potentially life-threatening situations. Britain's initial official policy of maintaining law and order throughout the country was gradually abandoned in favor of minimizing the risk to British troops. The task of securing lines of communication and designated routes of the eventual evacuation took precedence over maintaining law and order and preserving the status quo between Arabs and Jews.

The change was first felt in the south. On 28 February, the 61st Lorried Infantry Brigade, previously in charge of the south of the country (the northern Negev), was withdrawn from Palestine. It was replaced by a task force, Southforce, which consisted of an infantry battalion (2nd Battalion Kings Royal Rifle Corps) reinforced by a troop of armored cars (Life Guards), a battery of self-propelled antitank guns (M1), and a few auxiliary units.[11] At the time, one of the army's tasks was to secure the passage of eight weekly Jewish convoys.[12] Arab roadblocks in the village of Breir and the policy of avoiding direct confrontations with either side wherever possible led the army to concentrate its efforts on securing only the coastal road, deploying five daily patrols along it, thereby allowing Jews and Arabs to operate freely throughout the rest of the Negev. This allowed the Jews to found the settlement of Bror Hayil (18–19 April), opposite the Arab village of Breir, in an attempt to secure passage of Jewish convoys east of Breir and eventually to occupy a number of Arab villages before mid-May.[13]

The fact that the British Army followed an internally evolving policy, largely dictated by its own concerns and priorities rather than by a commonly suspected conspiracy to help one side against the other, proved a source of considerable confusion. Thus, the army's redeployment along the main Jerusalem–Latrun highway came as a surprise to the Jewish command, which had often accused the army of an anti-Jewish bias in its treatment of the Jerusalem convoys. On 23 February, the army decided to prohibit the regular use of the main road to Jerusalem, which had previously been designated as an evacuation route and therefore kept open to all traffic throughout the day (at night the road was under curfew). Previously, the British forces along the road were responsible for removing Arab roadblocks and extracting Jewish convoys held up by Arab ambushes. In addition, a military presence along the road was necessary to ensure the operation of the pumps of the water pipe to Jerusalem and maintenance work on the communication cables under the road, which remained the main telephone link of the government in Jerusalem with the rest of the country. However, an increasing rate of losses sustained by the army, the result of a steady improvement in Arab military effectiveness and consequent confidence, resulted in a decision to switch all road traffic beyond the bare minimum to the Beit Ur (Beit Horon) road, which ran through a homogeneous Arab-controlled area and therefore was not contested.

As a result, the Arab forces along the road were able to intensify their attacks on Jewish convoys,[14] with the result that by the end of March, the convoy system came to a halt. Hence, the British Army's decision to switch roads in order to reduce the threat to its soldiers from Arab attacks on Jewish convoys forced the Jewish forces onto the offensive in order to open the road to Jerusalem. This effort began with the Nachshon operation (3–15 April). By 15 May, the Hagana occupied the ridges and the Arab villages along the road between Bab-el-Wad and Jerusalem, thereby defeating the main Palestinian military force—the Eastern Brigade of the Holy Jihad—whose commander, Abdel Kader el-Husseini, was killed in the fighting.

For similar reasons, and after repeated attempts to secure a local cease-fire that would stabilize the situation until the final evacuation on 15 May, the army decided to withdraw from the mixed town of Safad[15] in which the Arabs enjoyed a clear demographic superiority. The army's commanders feared that a withdrawal from Safad would result in a massacre of its Jewish population. It offered to evacuate at least the civilian population under its protection, but the leaders of the Jewish community refused, and on 16 April, the army withdrew its sole undermanned company of Irish Guards from the town. However, contrary to expectations, the Jewish forces in Safad managed to withstand Arab attacks, and on 10 May occupied the town, with the result that its Arab population fled north to Lebanon.

In Tiberias, the Jews enjoyed a clear demographic and topographical advantage. The failure of the army commander in Tiberias to either broker or force a cease-fire led him to allow the Jewish forces to occupy the town on 19 April. The army arranged safe passage for the Arab population and stayed in Tiberias, now governed by the Jews, for another ten days, until its final withdrawal from the Galilee.

The army's decision to redeploy in the eastern Galilee culminated in its decision to withdraw its troops from most of the city of Haifa, leaving in its control a strip that included the port, from which the final evacuation of British troops in the north took place. As a result, the Jews occupied Haifa on 22 April, and the majority of the Arab population fled by sea and land with British armed protection.[16]

While allowing the two sides to fight it out between themselves as much as a month before the end of the Mandate, the British Army did not tolerate any action likely to endanger its lines of communication and its planned evacuation routes. In the Negev, an armored patrol shelled Kibbutz Mivtahim after Jewish armored cars attacked an Arab truck alongside an army roadblock on the coastal road near Rafah.[17] In Jerusalem, a faulty evaluation of British policy led Jewish troops to occupy the Arab neighborhood of Sheikh Jarrah, through which ran the main road from Jerusalem north and then west to Beit Ur and Latrun. The Jewish forces, having been warned repeatedly, were attacked and ejected from Sheikh Jarrah with the promise that when the Mandate ended, the neighborhood would be turned over to the Hagana. Similarly, stern army warnings prevented the Jews from following up their victory in Katamon in southern Jerusalem and occupying all of south Jerusalem, thereby threatening the southern evacuation route through Bethlehem and Hebron.

To conclude, the change in U.S. policy did not of itself change Jewish strategy, although it probably sharpened the sense of urgency with which the Yishuv prepared to face the ultimate military confrontation with the Arabs once the Mandate ended. Similarly, it may well have encouraged Arab leaders to believe that partition could still be prevented. But it was due to a series of unilateral British Army decisions to redeploy British troops with the purpose of reducing friction between them and the warring communities, in a way that would not compromise the final withdrawal at the end of the Mandate, that the war intensified between the Jews and Arabs. While the escalation was not generally of Jewish making, it both enabled and forced the Jewish forces to take the initiative, with the result that by the time the British Army withdrew from most of the country in mid-May, the Jewish partition state was a territorial reality and the Palestinian Arabs largely defeated. The Yishuv had realized the partition by its own military efforts earlier than it had anticipated. It was now faced with the daunting task of defending it against the invading regular Arab armies.

Notes

1. Yogev, *Political and Diplomatic Documents*, 474–75.
2. Ibid., 476.
3. Ibid., 477.
4. Rivlin and Orren, *War of Independence, Ben-Gurion's Diary*, entry for 20 March 1948.
5. Avizohar and Bareli, *Now or Never, Proceedings of Mapai*, 355.
6. Ibid., 356.
7. The full text is in Meser, *Hagana's Operational Plans 1937–1948*, 131.
8. Ibid., 132.
9. Ibid., 133.
10. Rivlin and Orren, *War of Independence, Ben-Gurion's Diary*, entry for 18 March 1948.
11. HQRA 1st Infantry Division Op. Instr. No. 5, 16.2.48, National Archives (UK), WO 261/722.
12. Southforce Operation Instruction 3, 28 February 1948, National Archives (UK), WO 261/755.
13. Mainly during Operation Barak by the Givati brigade.
14. See for example Sacha [Y. Alon] to Hagana H.Q., 7 March 1948, Israel Army Archive 922/75, 1026.
15. On the British Army's withdrawal from Safad, see Kadish, *British Army's Exit from Safed*. The main source on the subject is "Report on the events leading up to the evacuation of Safad town" by Lt. Col. D.M.L. Gordon Watson, C.O. of 1 Bn Irish Guards, Stockwell papers 6/125, Liddell Hart Centre for Military Archives.
16. On the British Army's decision to redeploy in Haifa, see Kadish, "British Army and the Evacuation of Haifa."
17. "History of the 4th Royal Tank Regiment, September 1974/ October 1949," 10–11. Ms. in the Tank Museum, Bevington, Dorset, UK.

Works Cited

Avizohar, Meir, and Avi Bareli, eds. *Now or Never, Proceedings of Mapai (The Labour Party of Eretz-Israel) in the Closing Year of the British Mandate.* [In Hebrew.] Beit Berl: Ayanot, 1989.

Kadish, Alon. "The British Army and the Evacuation of Haifa." In *Haifa in 1948*, edited by Y. Safron, 51–60. [In Hebrew.] Haifa: Haifa History Society, 2008.

———. The British Army's Exit from Safed. [In Hebrew.] Jerusalem: Ariel, 2006.

Meser, Oded. *Hagana's Operational Plans 1937–1948.* [In Hebrew.] Tel Aviv: Tag, 1996.

Rivlin, G., and E. Orren, eds. *The War of Independence, Ben-Gurion's Diary.* [In Hebrew.] Tel Aviv: Ministry of Defense Publication, 1983.

Yogev, Gadilia, ed. *Political and Diplomatic Documents, December 1947–May 1948.* [In Hebrew.]

Jerusalem: State of Israel, Israel State Archives/World Zionist Organization, Central Zionist Archives, 1979.

Archives
Israel Army Archive, Tel Hashomer, Israel
Liddel Hart Centre for Military Archives, King's College, London, UK
National Archives (UK), Richmond, Surrey, UK
Tank Museum, Bevington, Dorset, UK

The Soviet Union and the Establishment of Israel

Vladislav Zubok

THE SOVIET FACTOR IN THE ESTABLISHMENT of the State of Israel can best be described as the "Stalin factor." Without the Soviet angle, it is inconceivable to imagine how Israel could have emerged, at least in a diplomatic way, so successfully in 1948.

The scale and the various components of Soviet assistance to the Zionists was staggering in scale, in sharp contrast to the rising waves of anti-Semitism inside the Soviet Union. While the Kremlin was purging Jews from the security apparatus, the military, and the party institutions, and shutting down Yiddish-language cultural institutions in the Soviet Union and further afield, in its Eastern European empire it was trying to ally with the Zionist movement. How could this be?

There are several elements to consider in order to understand Stalinist foreign policy and its role in the emergence of Israel. First is the geopolitical goals of the Kremlin, colored by the Marxist-Leninist worldview. French scholar Laurent Rucker wrote, "Moscow concluded that if the Soviet Union was to succeed in weakening Great Britain in the Middle East, the Zionist movement was the only means of doing so."[1] The Soviet leaders, and Joseph Stalin himself, believed that the Middle East was an area of struggle between the leading imperialist powers, the United States and Britain. Soviet diplomacy had to exploit those controversies. They also believed that the Zionist movement was one of many movements of national liberation in the "gray zone" between the imperialist camp and the Soviet Union. As such, this movement could and should be supported by the Soviet Union as a tool against the British Empire to undermine it. At the same time, the Kremlin expected to do it without bringing American power into the region. Those assumptions affected Soviet foreign policy all the more as the Cold War was taking shape. Traces of these assumptions can be found in Soviet diplomatic correspondence and analytical papers.

Secondly, we have to consider the nature of Stalinist "realism" as it affected Soviet foreign policy calculations. Stalin's policies in the Mediterranean reflected the pattern of a Stalinist blend of Marxist-Leninist assumptions with the cynical Soviet realism, based on the idea of the immorality of world politics. Bolsheviks and Stalin believed that the interests of the "world proletariat" were identical to the interests of the Soviet Union and that the Kremlin could and should use any means, manipulate anything and anybody, to promote Soviet interests. This cynical realism of the Soviet leaders was to a great extent based on their reading of world history. For them, any foreign policy based on idealistic principles different from their own was either camouflage or stupidity. Paradoxically, this realism drove the Kremlin rulers to underestimate the other kinds of beliefs and ideological motivations of their opponents. Of course, Stalin often spoke of liberals and humanists as useful fools who could be exploited. Nevertheless, he discounted the beliefs of some of his partners, especially in the United States. Therefore, when Truman's religious beliefs later facilitated his recognition of Israel, this might have come as a surprise to Stalin. Viewed through Stalinist cynical lenses, the United States had little to gain from the ardent support of Israel, and this support, in contrast, complicated the U.S. relationship with the oil-rich Arab states in the Middle East.

Finally, we have to consider the impact of Stalin's personality and the impact of his cult on policy making. Stalin himself remains an enigmatic figure, despite many biographies and many revelations, including Simon Sebag Montefiore's recent biographies (*Young Stalin* and *Stalin: The Court of the Red Tsar*).[2] If we consider Stalin only in one dimension, his attitude towards Soviet Jews, we will never understand his actions on the Palestine issue in 1947/48. At best, we know that Stalin was very smart and had a lot of cunning. He cannot be gauged by simplistic measurements. Stalin held his cards so close and liked so much to keep his entourage uncertain about his real thinking that even his closest lieutenants did not know all elements of the game he played on the Palestine issue and Zionism. Moreover, Stalin seemed to enjoy surprising his entourage by his choices and decisions.

Unfortunately, we still have blank spots and many black holes in the Soviet record on this issue, despite the archival revelations of the last seventeen years. We also have not seen any records from the Soviet General Staff, nor do we have the intelligence records. I would be curious, for instance, to see the telegrams Stalin sent to the Kremlin from his vacation on the Black Sea in the fall of 1947.

When these documents become available, I hope we will find some tangible evidence on Stalin's thinking regarding Palestine and the support of Zionists there, as it evolved at that time.

Meanwhile, looking at the available records, I am puzzled by their silence regarding Jews. Even in the conversations of Stalin with foreigners (statesmen, diplomats, foreign communists, etc.), of which I have seen almost four hundred transcripts, I discovered that Stalin mentioned Palestine, Israel, Jews, Jewish issues, etc., extremely rarely. In one instance in October 1944, Churchill said to Stalin, "We are trying to persuade Jews to move to Libya, but they resist." So we know that they discussed Jews in October 1944 when they talked about a potential Soviet mandate to control Libya. Stalin mentioned Jews in December 1952. At that time, Stalin told the Politburo that all Jews are nationalists who support the British and Americans, that they expect Anglo-American capital to support them, and that they are all intelligence agents of the Anglo-American bloc.[3] What did Stalin really think about Jews? The purges of the Soviet security apparatus began at the end of the war, and in the foreign ministry they preceded the war. We can deduce that Stalin thought of Jews in multidimensional ways: both as a potential great tool in international affairs and a potential fifth column in domestic politics.[4]

My hypothesis is that Soviet support of Zionists, beginning in May 1947, was unthinkable without Stalin's personal decision, and this decision was driven by his pattern of probing Western powers, Great Britain, and the United States, in various parts of the Mediterranean and the Middle East, that is, the periphery of the Yalta "system" of spheres of influence. In 1945 Stalin demanded bases in Libya and on the Turkish Straits. In 1947/48, the Soviet leader sought to obtain bases in the region by supporting the Zionist movement and the establishment of an independent Jewish state. Until April 1947, Soviet diplomats suggested supporting a joint Jewish-Arab state for tactical reasons. However, Andrei Gromyko, on instructions from the Kremlin, demanded establishment of an independent Jewish state. It was not a cautious tactical game but rather a gamble, a probe that only Stalin could come up with. I would argue that this gamble was aimed at constructing a "socialist" Israel under Soviet tutelage, at using this new state to dislodge Britain from Palestine or, at best, to pit British interests against American interests in the Middle East.

It is often said that Stalin somehow underestimated the connection between the founders of Israel, the Zionists in Palestine, and American Jews. This was not the case at all. The available record from the Soviet Foreign Ministry demonstrates that all the experts there warned about exactly this, and predicted that Israel would inevitably gravitate towards the United States. And despite these warnings, the Kremlin master still decided to play out his gamble in Palestine. What considerations made Stalin brush aside the cautious and prudent expertise? Most obviously, the fate of his previous geopolitical probes in the region must have influenced Stalin's mind. His humiliating retreat from Iran in 1946 and the unsuccessful pressures on Turkey may have created a psychological background that magnified the temptation for the Kremlin dictator to recoup influence in Palestine, even against high odds. Also, Stalin's determination to make another probe in the Mediterranean could have been boosted by his past successes in using national liberation movements, including those in the Middle East. For example, he was quite successful in creating and supporting the Kurdish and Azeri national movements in 1945 to 1946 in northern Iran. Only the stubbornness of the Iranian government and the joint actions by Great Britain and the United States prevented the Soviet Union from gaining a sphere of influence and access to Iranian oil in 1946.[5]

The Soviet Union had considerable cultural and intelligence assets among the Jews, including those living in Palestine. Most of them, after all, had come from the Russian Empire, and support for the Soviet Union (at least some aspects of Soviet experiment) among them was high. Millions of Jews, including Zionist leaders in the West, worshipped the Soviet Army, recognizing its important contribution to the defeat of Nazism. Stalin had reason to expect that Soviet support of the Zionist cause would increase even further the already high number of "agents of influence" in Palestine who would advocate Israel's pro-Soviet orientation. Indeed, Gromyko's declaration in May 1947 in support of an independent Jewish state caused a sensation and earned much gratitude among influential Jewish groups in the United States.

By that time, the Zionists had no international support for the idea of creating an independent state of Israel, and even the Truman administration, including the president himself, was hesitant on this issue. Gromyko's speech created a new international dynamic that favored Zionists' plans. The Soviet-Zionist collaboration developed by leaps and bounds. In October 1947, just weeks after the establishment of the Cominform (Communist Information Bureau) in Poland, Gromyko's deputy Semen Tsarapkin gave a speech at the UN supporting the separation of Jewish and Arab states in Palestine. On 29 November, the USSR, as well as Ukraine and Belorussia, cast three votes for the separation scheme. In December 1947, as the Soviet Union and its communist satellites in Europe were busy attacking the Marshall Plan as the scheme of American subjugation of Europe, American Zionists held a series of secret meetings with Tsarapkin and Gromyko. In direct outcome of these meetings, the Czechoslovak government (still independent from Moscow, but with the communists in control of the Ministry of Defense) stopped sending armaments to the Arabs and, jointly with communist Yugoslavia, created a secret channel to deliver "trophy" German weapons (surplus weapons produced by Czech plants for the Third Reich) to Hagana. The communist coup in Czechoslovakia had no influence on this channel. Deliveries of arms to Israel from the communist camp continued until 1951.

One potentially interesting way to think about Stalin's calculations in Palestine is that the Kremlin leader did not expect the war between the Arabs and the Jews to end so decisively in favor of Israel. The evidence supporting this hypothesis, as always, is indirect. In August 1948, Soviet diplomat Yakov Malik, in conversation with Moshe Sharett, expressed great admiration and surprise at the Jewish victory.[6] If we imagine an alternative historical scenario, if the Jews in Palestine had not won such a decisive victory, they instead would have required support from outside. Stalin's backing of an independent Jewish state would have then been a much more influential factor. Until we gain access to additional sources, Stalin's scenario of having a weak Jewish state under his tutelage cannot be corroborated or rejected. At the same time, a weak Israel always on the brink of collapse would have been definitely much more dependent on Soviet support.

Stalin always tried to play many chess games simultaneously; he was always thinking about several disparate policies at once. The Soviet policies regarding Palestine cannot be examined in isolation from other issues that were evolving simultaneously. The growing role of the United States in the Mediterranean, beginning with the Truman Doctrine, and its use of the powerful economic-financial card after proclamation of the Marshall Plan could not help forcing Stalin to make countermoves. As the bipolarity in Europe and elsewhere increased, the role of Jews as a joker card in Stalin's foreign policy increased. It would have been a tremendous victory for Soviet foreign policy if Jewish interests had aligned with those of the Soviet Union.

Stalin had used the Jewish card several times earlier. In 1942, during the worst moments of the war with Germany, Stalin created the Jewish Anti-Fascist Committee that appealed to the Jews around the world. So, one can consider that in 1947/48, the Kremlin dictator decided again to play the Jewish card. And then, of course, came those surprises I mentioned, above all, Israel's decisive military victory in 1948. Another surprise, although it is based on extremely tenuous evidence, was Truman's decision to support Israel. Of course, the United States and the Soviet Union ruled on parallel tracks, competing for the soul of the Jewish people as they had competed for the soul of Germans. Nevertheless, Stalin did not expect Truman to act as quickly as he did. The factors that might be considered in this case include Truman's religious beliefs as well as domestic politics. Although Stalin himself was kicked out of a seminary, he consistently dismissed the role of religious beliefs. He conceived himself as a realist, he was proud of his own cynical realism and rationality, but he never understood how people like Truman could act on their beliefs, nor on other kinds of more materialistic interests.

In May 1948, many Jews, including the founders of Israel, felt considerable gratitude to the Soviet Union and to Stalin for their role in the establishment of Israel. There were many interesting manifestations of this gratitude in the archival documentation, and most were unofficial. In September 1949, Israel's Ukrainian-born foreign minister, Moshe Sharett, wrote to the Israeli ambassador in London, Mordechai Eliash, resisting the latter's proposal that Israel take sides in the Cold War by joining the democratic nations opposed to the USSR. Sharett wrote, "This would be blatant ingratitude towards the USSR and its allies, especially considering the inestimable political and practical assistance provided for us during the decisive phase of our struggle for independence."[7]

It was Stalin who helped the Israeli statesmen and Jewish public opinion step over the feeling of gratitude to the USSR. The Kremlin dictator was probably the least likely person to capitalize on anybody's gratitude. He was known for squandering his capital of gratitude everywhere in the world, and that was the case with Israel. He had some hopes of using Israel as a pawn in his geopolitical game until 1950/51. Then, with the outbreak of the Korean War and the remarkable success of NATO, that hope faded. One can imagine his anger growing, which is reflected in the increasing anti-Semitism in the Soviet Union beginning in 1947 and 1948. The final straw was his realization that Israel was unusable as a Jewish political asset. Israel was definitely allied with the other side, despite the wishes of such men as Sharett. At that moment, Stalin's policy towards Israel and Jews was no longer the product of complex Machiavellian calculations, but rather the result of the brutal, repressive, and vindictive mind-frame. In January 1953, the aged dictator unleashed the infamous Kremlin doctor's affair and, some historians believe, triggered preparations for a state-sponsored massive pogrom against Jews in the Soviet Union. These preparations were aborted only by Stalin's death.

Notes

1. Rucker, "Moscow's Surprise," 35.
2. Published by Alfred A. Knopf, 2007 and 2004, respectively.

3. Dnevnik, "Malysheva."
4. See Milstein, *Skvoz gody voin i nishchety.*
5. Hasanli, *Yuzhnii Azerbaijan.*
6. Kolokolov, *Sovetsko-izrailskie otnosheniia.*
7. *Sovetsko-izrailskie otnosheniia,* 2:67–68.

Works Cited

Dnevnik V. A. "Malysheva." *Istochnik* 5 (1997): 103–47.

Hasanli, Jamil P. *Yuzhnii Azerbaijan: Nachalo kholodnoi voiny.* Baku: Adiolgli, 2003.

Kolokolov, B. L., ed., *Sovetsko-izrailskie otnosheniia: Sbornik dokumentov,* vol. 1. Moscow: Mezhdunarodnye Otnosheniia, 2000.

Milstein, Mikhail. *Skvoz gody voin i nishchety. Vospominaniia voiennogo razvedchika.* Moscow: ITAR-TASS, 2000.

Montefiore, Simon Sebag. *Stalin: The Court of the Red Tsar.* New York: Alfred A. Knopf, 2004.

———. *Young Stalin.* New York: Alfred A. Knopf, 2007.

Rucker, Laurent. "Moscow's Surprise: The Soviet-Israeli Alliance of 1947–1949." Cold War International History Project, Working Paper # 46.

The U.S. Army, Displaced Persons, and American Palestine Policy

Ronald W. Zweig

POSTWAR AMERICAN POLICY ON PALESTINE EVOLVED in response to different concerns in Washington, in Europe, and in the Middle East. The policy that emerged—American support for partition and American refusal to collaborate with any British attempt to impose a binational solution on Palestine—was a result of prolonged wrangling between opposing forces within the American government: the White House on one side and the State Department and the Department of War (which represented the U.S. occupation forces in Europe) on the other. The Truman administration was motivated both by a real sympathy for the Jewish survivors of the Holocaust and by the need to win elections for the Democratic Party, at every level of government, in order to establish the legitimacy of a president who had not himself been elected. This has all been extensively documented. The role of the State Department, of Secretaries of State James Byrnes and George Marshall, both of whom were unsympathetic to Zionism and to the Jewish settlement's drive towards independence, and especially of Loy Henderson, director of the Office of Near East and African Affairs within the State Department, who was actively hostile to Zionism, have also been very well documented. This essay will explore the third factor in American policy making: the role of the U.S. occupation forces in Europe. This role is much less discussed, but was an absolutely crucial factor in the evolution of American policy towards the Jewish issue as a whole, both to Palestine and to the Jewish displaced persons.

To understand the position of the American forces as they liberated Western and Central Europe and then took over responsibility for the American zones of occupation in Germany and Austria, it is necessary to acknowledge certain facts about World War II. During the struggle to defeat Hitler, the Allies did not divert their attention from the larger aim of winning the war by making any serious attempt to save Jews or other victims of the Holocaust. They also failed to correctly anticipate the number and condition of the Jews who would survive after the war. Their wartime planning for the postwar era—the assessment of what awaited the Allied forces when they liberated Europe—was sorely lacking. In all the extensive Allied planning on how they would handle the administration of civilian populations, no attention was given to the fact that a significant population of Jewish survivors would be liberated by the Allies from the camps. In fact, it was generally assumed that there would be no survivor population, because it was believed that all the Jews had been deported to Poland and murdered there. But that assumption was wrong. Ultimately, the American, British, and French liberated between 70,000 and 100,000 Jewish survivors from the large network of concentration camps, slave labor camps, and satellite camps (over 1,600 such camps were liberated in Western and Central Europe). Nobody had anticipated that such a large number of Jews would be liberated, and nobody had anticipated that their needs would be dramatically different from the needs of the other displaced persons, refugees, freed prisoners of war, and slave laborers, who everybody knew would be found in large numbers in liberated Europe. The situation of total unpreparedness was so widespread that when British Army units entered Bergen-Belsen and discovered 14,000 Jews, most of who were in urgent need of hospitalization, all they had available to offer immediate help were fifty folding beds and eight army nurses. When the British forces realized how badly they had miscalculated, they immediately mobilized large medical resources and made a heroic effort to improve the situation in the weeks and months that followed. But this general state of unpreparedness in dealing with the critical situation of the survivors in the first weeks after liberation was characteristic of all the Allied armies, and had serious consequences for the frailest of the liberated camp internees.

The second point is that the Allies also misunderstood the nature of the Jewish survivor population. As the Allies advanced, they were aware of the fact that they would liberate a large number of concentration camp internees (non-Jewish), all of whom, it was considered, were a threat to civil order and public health. So, as the Allied armies progressed, one of the first steps they took was to seal down the camps to ensure that the internee population would not mingle with the German civil population so as to avoid the probable spread of typhus, which was rife in the camps and was the great fear of all armies on the move.

It was also felt that the liberated internees would create severe problems of law and order, including taking revenge against the German civilian population, looting of food, and so on. So it was decided that the Allies would keep the liberated internees in the camps. They would be supplied with adequate food and medicine and so on, but internees would not be allowed out. As a result of this policy, in the months of April, May, and the beginning of June 1945, as Europe was liberated and the war in Europe came to an end, one of the strongest images left to us is of the concentration camp survivors, Jews and non-Jews, still in their filthy pajama-uniforms, under guard behind barbed wire. Only now, the guards were American and British, not Germans. In fact, at first German and Austrian Jewish survivors were defined as "enemy aliens" and were treated like the German civil population (entitled to only reduced rations). It took weeks for the Allied administrations to adjust from this mind-set to an understanding that these were Holocaust survivors who needed special treatment and long-term rehabilitation, and deserved to be treated better than the German civilian population.

All of this made very bad press back in Washington. In addition, there was the embarrassment of George Patton. A war hero, Patton was also an anti-Semite, and in two scurrilous press conferences he assailed the survivors—"those dirty, lazy people" in the camps—and said America should actually be aligning with those "fine blond soldiers of the Waffen SS in the prisoner of war camps" in order to fight the Russians.[1] This did not go down well in Washington either. By the summer of 1945, there was considerable public criticism in Washington of the behavior of the American military towards the survivors.

President Truman responded by sending a Committee of Inquiry to Europe. The committee was led by Earl Harrison, a professor of constitutional law and a specialist on immigration and refugee matters at the University of Pennsylvania. Truman sent Harrison to Europe to investigate the condition of the Jewish survivors in the camps and to recommend future policy. Harrison did not go alone; he was accompanied by three people who had extensive experience with refugee affairs: Patrick Malin, a Quaker and vice director of the Intergovernmental Committee on Refugees, Herbert Katzki of the War Refugee Board and the American Jewish Joint Distribution Committee (the Joint), and Joseph Schwartz, the leader of the Joint in Europe. Apparently, Joseph Schwartz actually drafted the Harrison Report and he used extremely harsh language. The report stated that it would appear to the survivors that the American army was treating the Jewish survivors of the Holocaust in the same way that the Nazis treated them, except for the fact they weren't killing them. That was an outrageous statement and it was designed to attract attention. The report then went on to make two crucial recommendations. The first was that Jews and non-Jews be separated in the displaced persons (DP) camps, because many of the non-Jews that were displaced persons in the summer of 1945 were in fact Nazi collaborators. They remained in the DP camps because they could not go back to their homes in Eastern Europe. As there was obvious friction with the Jews in the camps, the first thing the Harrison Report recommended was that there should be separate Jewish camps for the survivors of the Holocaust. This was of major significance. The next point, no less significant, was that Harrison repeated the standard demand of the Zionists and of all Jewish organizations, that the British immediately issue 100,000 immigration certificates for the Holocaust survivors so that they could go to Palestine.

Had the British accepted this recommendation in the summer of 1945, it is doubtful whether the State of Israel would have come into existence in 1948. The subsequent pressure of DPs seeking to reach Palestine, resulting in the phenomenon of illegal immigration and the conflict between Holocaust survivors and the British Navy, would never have occurred. In late August 1945, when the Harrison Report was published, there were not even 100,000 survivors in the camps. Many had died in the months after liberation. Others, from Western and Central European countries, had returned to their homes. By the late summer of 1945 there were probably no more than 50,000 Jews in the camps. Nevertheless, the figure of 100,000 had become the oft-repeated mantra of Zionist public relations, and it was adopted by Harrison—giving it the aura of a demand that was not only frequently repeated but now also semiofficial.

The impact of the Harrison Report was huge. Eisenhower, commander in chief of the American forces in Europe, realized that the manner in which his forces were managing the Jewish survivor issue was a public relations disaster for the army. The only way to assuage public criticism in Washington was to accept Harrison's recommendations. The U.S. occupation forces in Germany and Austria faced many more pressing issues, but while the Jewish issue was marginal, it was also a lightning rod for public opinion in America. Its very marginality was the answer: it would be possible to concede to Jewish demands concerning the management of the DP camps without impinging on the real concerns of the U.S. forces. And so, in October 1945, when David Ben-Gurion visited American forces in Europe and the survivors of the Holocaust, the army was able to agree to his requests. The first was that the Jewish DPs be placed in separate camps. The second was that Jewish organizations (the Jewish Agency and the Joint), together with the survivors, be allowed to run their own camps. The third request was that the American army would allow Jews who were fleeing anti-Semitism as well as Communism in Eastern Europe to enter the American zones of occupation in Germany and Austria. The British were not sympathetic to these people, so the American army would have achieved a public relations coup if they agreed to allow them refuge. Eisenhower was able to agree to these demands, but not to Ben-Gurion's final demand: if the Jews were to have separate camps with Jewish administration, why not create a temporary Jewish autonomous zone in Bavaria, with a Jewish flag, until Palestine became a Jewish state? This latter request was rejected out of hand.

Following the Harrison Report's criticism of the army, an adviser on Jewish affairs was appointed to the American officer commanding in Europe. The adviser's function was to act as a liaison between the army and the DPs, and between the army and the Jewish organizations in Washington. He wore an American army uniform, had the rank of an officer, but also had to work with the Jewish organizations, be fluent in Yiddish, have a working knowledge of Hebrew, and be able to deal with the refugees. Stung by the public criticism of its behavior towards the Jews, the army now had in place a policy and an apparatus whereby Jewish needs could be met without unduly taxing the military government in Germany and Austria.

Slowly, the number of Jews in the camps began to grow. Between 70,000 and 100,000 had been liberated in March through May 1945. By summer, 50,000 were left in the camps, and from then on the numbers slowly grew with the influx of Jews from Eastern Europe. Jewish life in the camps revived, and under a now sympathetic military administration, Jewish education commenced (with teachers from Palestine), and Jewish newspapers were printed, although there was no newsprint available for general German newspapers. In a symbolic gesture indicating the revival of Jewish life in Europe, an edition of the Talmud was even produced in the camps. The Jewish Agency for Palestine and the Joint were allowed to administer the camps, now exclusively reserved for Jewish DPs. The result of these developments was the one thing the British did not want: a revival of Jewish collective identity and its political expression—Zionism. In fact, there was very strong Zionist activity in the camps. By 1946, an increasing number of the Jewish displaced persons stated that they wanted to go to Palestine. Gradually, the Palestine orientation of the DPs grew and with it, the British concern about the implications of the growing number of Holocaust survivors in the DP camps in the American zones of occupation. Clearly, this emerging situation would have major implications for Britain's attempts to find a long-term solution to the Arab-Jewish conflict in Palestine.

The Jewish DP population was still a small percentage of the overall DPs, about 10 percent, but the number of non-Jews in the camps was declining and the number of Jews was growing. There were plenty of places for the non-Jews to go: Britain, Brazil, South Africa, Australia, New Zealand, etc. However, none of these places was sympathetic to Jewish immigration. The State Department tried hard to resettle DPs and reduce the numbers in the camps, but in one very humiliating case two ships carrying Jewish DPs were sent to Brazil only to be returned to Europe when the immigration authorities there realized that the passengers were Jewish. One can sense the growing exasperation about Jewish refugee rehabilitation in the records of the State Department. Efforts to find alternative venues for resettlement other than Palestine were gradually abandoned. At the same time that the Jewish DP population was growing in the American zones of occupation, the number of American troops in the U.S. zones was actually declining. In fact, although the American zones of occupation in Germany and Austria were much larger than the British zones of occupation, the Americans maintained only 20 percent as many soldiers in occupied Europe as did the British. In other words, the Americans were understaffed. As a result, they gave the task of policing the borders of Germany to the newly reconstituted German police force. German police with American weapons were supposed to guard the borders against all infiltrators, including Jews seeking protection from anti-Semitism and Communism in Eastern Europe. This was a delicate situation with the makings of another public relations disaster for the U.S. occupation authorities. They could not allow the German police to forcibly stop Jews seeking protection from crossing the border of Germany. The Jews were in any case only a very small proportion of the overall illegal border crossings, some 10 to 15 percent. But it was the most sensitive politically and instructions were issued that the Germans should turn a blind eye to Jews crossing into American-controlled territory. By December 1945, the flow of Jews out of Poland alone into the United States zone was over five hundred a day. There was a serious question of whether the Soviets were actively pushing them out of Poland in order to embarrass the Americans in Germany. Later on, it became clear that Jewish organizations were organizing the migration westwards. That was a manageable number, and in the spring of 1946 the State Department enlisted the help of Jewish organizations in Washington to maintain the level and regulate the flow. The U.S. agreed to allow the influx to continue on condition that this fact was not flaunted publicly. Parties of Jews entering the American zones were to be kept smaller than one hundred—even if this meant simply the façade of breaking up larger groups and sending them across the border at brief intervals. The organizations were happy to comply.

Nevertheless, during the summer of 1946, the general displaced persons problem (about one million people were still in camps) was becoming increasingly burdensome. By June 1946, 3,000 officers and enlisted men were fully engaged in looking after the displaced persons and a further 74,000 army personnel spent at least 10 percent of their time in logistical support. The food, clothing, and shelter for the displaced persons cost the United States taxpayer $8 million per month. At the same time, in the summer of 1946, the Jewish DP population reached 90,000 and was growing steadily. An alarmed telegram to Washington by General Mark Clark, the officer commanding the American forces in Austria, reported that between 350,000 and 750,000 Jewish refugees were expected to leave their homes in the summer and autumn of 1946, with a majority migrating into the U.S. zones. Clark, supported by his counterpart in Germany, General Joseph McNarney, asked Washington to allow them to close the borders. But every time they requested authority from the Truman administration to close the borders, they were turned down for domestic political and for humanitarian reasons. Washington repeatedly refused to allow the closure of the borders of the American zones to Jewish refugees from Eastern Europe.

Washington's oversight of the administration of civilian affairs in the occupied zones was the responsibility of General John Hilldring in the State Department in Washington, assisted by his second in command, Herbert Fierst. Hilldring charged Fierst, among other tasks, with responsibility for all Jewish affairs in the occupied zones. Fierst came from an American Jewish family with strong Zionist roots. (He showed me his bar mitzvah photo, held in Jerusalem in the early 1930s, with his grandfather on one side of the thirteen-year-old boy and Chaim Nahman Bialik on the other. Clearly this was a family with standing in the Zionist world.) In the spring of 1946, the situation changed dramatically in Poland. Almost 200,000 Polish Jews were allowed to return to Poland from the Soviet Union. But in July of that year there was a major pogrom in Kielce, Poland, and within a month, tens of thousands of Jews packed their bags and headed westward to the American zone. Between August and October 1946, 90,000 Jews left Poland, followed by thousands more in the months that followed. This was exactly the crisis the Americans were worried about.

Already in November 1945, the American and British governments agreed to form a joint committee to examine the future of Palestine and also the future of the Jewish DPs in Europe. The Anglo-American Committee of Inquiry issued its report in April 1946. The report was unimpressive and with a single exception, none of its many recommendations had any serious impact. However, that one recommendation was to have huge historical importance: as with the

Harrison Report, the Joint Committee called for the immediate release of 100,000 immigration certificates to Palestine. One of the American conditions for joining the British in this Committee of Inquiry was that if the conclusions were unanimous, the British government would commit itself to implementing the recommendations. So when the committee unanimously called for 100,000 immigration certificates to Palestine, the American army seriously believed that the Jewish DP problem was about to be resolved. Planning began in a very efficient manner for the migration to Palestine of the displaced persons and the closure of the camps. American officers began planning the movement of 100,000 of the DPs to the ports of Marseille and Genoa by train, where ships would transport them to Palestine. American army plans were drawn up to create tent camps for the DPs when they reached Palestine. The plans were detailed and ready for immediate implementation. After all, the British government had agreed to adopt any recommendation made unanimously by the Joint Committee.

In June, talks were held in London to implement the recommendations. The U.S. Army sent officers from Germany and Austria to London with the shipping plans and train schedules. Everything was set to go. But the British reneged on their commitment, explaining that the maintenance of law and order in Palestine would be disrupted by the influx of another 100,000 Jews. The diplomatic consequences of these developments in Anglo-American relations were complex and are not relevant here. For the U.S. military in Europe, however, the inability to implement their plans for the resettlement of 100,000 survivors caused a turning point in the army's willingness to collaborate with the British on all matters relating to the DP problem. In June 1946, there were 133,000 Jewish refugees in the American zones of occupation, and 116,000 had said they wanted to go to Palestine. If the army could have resettled 100,000 of them, it would have been able to close almost all the DP camps in its care. But British backtracking on their firm commitment prevented this from happening, and the U.S. occupation authorities were apparently stuck with a problem that was getting more onerous by the day.

Discreetly, the army now began an unofficial policy of cooperation with the organizers of illegal immigration to Palestine, with the full backing of Hilldring and Fierst in Washington. Just as the army had been instructed to allow the continued infiltration of Jews into the American zones from Eastern Europe, they were now willing to facilitate the "exfiltration" (a word coined in army documents)[2] of Jews out of their zones. Although this does not concur with the heroic mythology of the organizers of illegal immigration, who like to believe that they were involved in a dangerous and illicit operation, in reality they received the tactical cooperation and encouragement of the occupation army. In the twenty-two months following the failed talks in London, almost 50 percent of the illegal immigration—35,000 out of the 72,000 total illegal immigrants that came to Palestine from 1945 to 1948—originated in the American zones of occupation. And it is, of course, inconceivable that 35,000 people could move illegally against the wishes of the U.S. occupation forces. By encouraging "exfiltration," the United States unintentionally became an accomplice in the developments that facilitated the partition of Palestine. By permitting the *Bricha,* or the movement of Jews from Eastern Europe to Central Europe, by allowing the independence of the Jewish displaced persons camps, which in turn facilitated strengthening of Jewish identity, and by allowing the movement of DPs out of Germany and Austria on their way to becoming illegal immigrants into Palestine, the United States played a key role in the events leading to Israel's independence.

Notes

1. Patton's sympathy to the Germans and objections to denazification, his hostility to the Russians, and his anti-Semitism are discussed extensively by all his biographers. See, for example, Blumenson, Patton, ch. 9; Axelrod, *Patton,* ch. 13; and Hirshson, *General Patton,* ch. 18.
2. The term "exfiltration" appeared frequently in U.S. Army policy documents from 1947. See, for example, Philip Bernstein to General Huebner, Chief of Staff, EUCOM, 25 March 1947, "Memo: Denial of Displaced Persons Care to Future Applicants," National Archives, RG260, OMGUS, Adjutant-General Decimal Files, 383.7; or Minutes of Adjutant-General Office meeting, 4 April 1947, "Termination of Admissions to UNDP Assembly Centers," National Archives, RG260, OMGUS, Adjutant-General Decimal Files, 383.7.

Works Cited

Axelrod, Alan. *Patton: A Biography.* New York: Palgrave Macmillan, 2006.
Blumenson, Martin. *Patton: The Man Behind the Legend, 1885–1945.* New York: Morrow, 1985.
Hirshson, Stanley P. *General Patton: A Soldier's Life.* New York: HarperCollins, 2002.

Archives

National Archives (US), Washington, DC, USA

Why Did President Truman Support the Establishment of the State of Israel?

Introduction to Session 3

William A. Brown

The subject of Truman and the Jews, especially Truman and American Jews, has been considered in numerous studies, and I've found the issue fascinating. I'm struck by the relationship between Truman and his wartime buddy Eddie Jacobson, and the impact of that relationship on Truman's decision to support and recognize the State of Israel. It is well documented and was a significant relationship. However, I think there has been a tendency to overly concentrate on that one friendship. In my own reading, which is based in part on online access to the Harry S. Truman Library archives in Independence, Missouri, I find snippets of other relationships I would like to share with you.

In Michael Beschloss's article in the 14 May 2008 issue of *Newsweek* magazine on presidential courage, he refers to the Jewish Viner family who lived next door to the Trumans in Independence for a couple of years. In an interview with Sarah Viner that is available in a Jewish community center in Kansas City, she said that during Shabbat he was the "Shabbas goy" for the family household chores.[1] I have another one and that is fascinating to me: I'm 99 percent sure that another critical person in Truman's early life and career was Jewish. That person is Ted Marks. Theodore Marks was born in Liverpool, immigrated to the United States around 1904 or 1906, and came to Kansas City as a tailor. He joined the Missouri National Guard and when his application was being taken, his interviewer was a corporal, Harry S. Truman, who joked, "You speak a pretty good English for a guy who's been here only six months...."[2] They were in an artillery outfit in the Missouri National Guard when President Wilson sent General "Black Jack" Pershing to cope with Pancho Villa's terrorist raids on the Mexican border. Ted went to Mexico with an artillery unit of the Missouri National Guard and rose to become first sergeant of his battery. He came back to Kansas City, took up tailoring again, and made Harry Truman's suits. As World War I approached, they both became commissioned officers. They went to France together; Harry commanded Battery

D in action in France, and Ted Marks commanded Battery C. Harry married Bess Wallace shortly after returning from France as a local hero. At the wedding, his best man was Ted Marks, who may have been raised as a non-Jew or secular Jew. In any event, I find it really remarkable, given the fact that although Harry Truman grew up in Missouri, where there was a considerable amount of anti-Semitism, that he had many Jewish friends and contacts. Therefore, to focus solely on his relationship with Eddie Jacobson as the defining experience in his attitude towards Jews and Israel is, I think, a bit overemphasized.

The two papers in this session look at the character of President Truman. Ronald and Allis Radash have been working on a book-length manuscript on Truman and Israel for several years. They present conclusions from their extensive research and suggest that President Truman, in recognizing the State of Israel in 1948, may have acted differently than his predecessor Franklin Roosevelt would have. Their paper looks at four key Jewish American men who influenced Truman. Michael Cohen, the author of a 1990 book on Truman and Israel finds Truman less impacted by moral concerns and directed by domestic political motives in the presidential election year of 1948.

Notes
1. Schulte, *Mid-America's Promise*, 32–33.
2. Quoted in McCullough, *Truman*, 109.

Works Cited
McCullough, David. *Truman*. New York: Simon and Schuster, 1992.
Schulte, Joseph, ed. *Mid-America's Promise: A Profile of Kansas City Jewry*. Kansas City, MO: Jewish Community Foundation, 1982.

Truman, Jews, and Zionists

Ronald Radosh and Allis Radosh

When David Ben-Gurion proclaimed the creation of Israel on 14 May 1948, President Harry S. Truman immediately announced that the United States would grant *de facto* recognition to the new Jewish state. David Niles, who stayed on as Special Assistant for Minority Affairs when Truman assumed the presidency, believed that had Franklin D. Roosevelt lived, he would not have taken that step. What led Truman, who had pledged to follow and carry out FDR's foreign policy, to reach a conclusion so different than the man whose policies he sought to emulate?

This paper explores the part played by the Zionist movement in America, and then examines the impact that four American Jewish men—children of Eastern European Jewish immigrants who did not belong to any Zionist organization—had on Truman's decision. Three of them—Samuel I. Rosenman, David K. Niles, and Max Lowenthal—worked for Truman in the White House, either on his staff or as an adviser. The fourth was his old friend and former business partner, Eddie Jacobson. We don't claim that Truman made the decisions he did because of these men, only that without their presence, commitment, and intercession, the result might have been different.

Hitler's rise to power in Germany and escalating attacks on European Jewry coincided with Truman's own rise to political power when in 1935, at the age of fifty, he was elected to the U.S. Senate. The Missouri senator was in the Democratic Party's mainstream when he denounced Hitler's campaign against the Jews, wrote letters for his Jewish constituents trying to get their friends and relatives out of Europe, and joined the American Christian Palestine Committee, headed by his Senate colleague Robert F. Wagner. Loyal to FDR, Truman followed his prescription that the best path for saving the Jews was to win the war, but that "when the right time comes I am willing to help make the fight for a Jewish homeland in Palestine."[1]

Truman learned about the terrible fate of the Jews along with the rest of the American public in April of 1945. General Dwight D. Eisenhower, shocked by what he saw as he toured the liberated camps, invited American newspaper reporters and editors, senators and congressmen, to fly to Europe from the United States to see it for themselves. "The barbarous treatment these people received in the German concentration camps," Eisenhower told them, "is almost unbelievable." He made available to the press all the resources of his command so the American people would learn why their men had been fighting.[2] The press reports and the newsreel footage gave Truman nightmares. "It was a horrible thing," he told *CBS News* in 1964. "I saw and I dream about it even to this day."[3]

When FDR chose Truman to run as his vice president, the expectation was that, due to FDR's declining health, the Missouri senator would ultimately become president. This prediction came true on 12 April 1945. Truman felt unprepared to step into FDR's shoes and was insecure about many things, but after his years in the Senate, he was confident that he could find a just solution for the situation of the Jewish survivors and the promises made to them after the First World War for a homeland in Palestine. He did not anticipate the maelstrom he was about to enter. Palestine became, his daughter, Margaret, pointed out, "the most difficult dilemma of his entire administration."[4] Truman soon found himself caught up in conflicts over these issues with his own State and Defense establishment, the British, the Arabs, Congress and other American politicians, and the American Jewish community, especially its organized Zionists. Sympathetic though Truman was to the abstract idea of a Jewish homeland in Palestine, when he assumed the presidency, the State Department quickly convinced him that any moves in that direction would require American troops and might start a new world war. He decided to focus instead on the short-term goal of helping the European Jewish refugees in DP camps find new homes and rebuild their broken lives in Palestine, where the majority of them said they wanted to go. This humanitarian crusade to help the refugees go to Palestine was popular with American Jews and the public at large, and was supported by American military administrators in Europe who could not keep the DPs in the camps indefinitely.

That Truman was unable to accomplish this rather modest goal was a political failure that his opponents exploited. As Truman later acknowledged, the British held the Mandate over Palestine and controlled immigration, and they rejected Truman's entreaties to let the refugees in. Truman's demands on the British opened a Pandora's box and led to a chain of events that he did not anticipate nor could entirely control. The British met Truman's request with a suggestion that the two countries form a joint Anglo-American Committee to look into the problem. When no satisfactory solution resulted, the war-weary and financially strapped British decided to give up the Mandate and take the issue to the United Nations.

After the war, the American Jewish community was, by default, the largest and wealthiest Jewish community in the world. The Jews had prospered as never before in pluralistic and democratic America. Zionism had been a small minority movement before the war. The Jewish establishment, by and large, thought the idea of a Jewish state unnecessary, even dangerous. It would threaten their status as Americans and make them suspect as having dual loyalties. But the Holocaust caused many American Jews to become increasingly sympathetic to the Zionists' goals, even if they were not active members of the Zionist movement. The inability of the Western democracies to save their fellow Jews from the gas chambers and to give them a safe haven, and their refusal even now to admit the survivors, strengthened the Zionists' argument that the Jews would only be safe once they had their own country and could defend themselves. Those American Jews who became sympathetic did not want this other country for themselves, but as Eddie Jacobson wrote to Truman, for "my suffering people across the seas."[5]

Public opinion polls, and support by influential journalists and politicians of every political stripe, showed that a large segment of the American public had come to support the Zionists. A good deal of this support resulted from the efforts of Zionist organizations which, in 1939, had formed an umbrella group, the American Zionist Emergency Council (AZEC), to coordinate their activities. By 1945, AZEC's driving force was its militant leader, Rabbi Abba Hillel Silver of Cleveland, who rejected the Jews' long tradition of using personal diplomacy with the powers that be to make their case and protect their people. Silver's rival, Rabbi Stephen Wise, had been the Jewish leader closest to Roosevelt, but the late president's promises to him that the Jews would receive justice if they were patient and waited for the war to be won, had not been realized. Silver was not going to let the new president mollify them with empty promises.

Silver called for a change in the Zionists' approach. He argued that in a democracy, the people had a right to raise their voices and would have to be listened to. He believed that both major political parties should be made to vie for Jewish support and that it was a mistake to be in the pocket of the Democratic Party and thus be taken for granted.[6] To the chagrin of the Democrats, including Roosevelt and Truman, Silver proceeded to form a close alliance with Republican Senator Robert A. Taft of Ohio, a supporter of Zionist goals. Silver, a gifted organizer and orator, approached this task with zeal. "With the help of 400-odd local Zionist emergency councils throughout the country," wrote Silver's friend and closest associate, Emanuel Neumann, "we kept up an unceasing campaign on a hundred fronts. Letters and telegrams by the hundreds of thousands were sent to the State Department and to the White House. Countless mass meetings and conferences were held; open letters were published in the newspapers; marches, parades, and open-air demonstrations were arranged. Repeated appeals were made to the conscience of America, to the churches and the labor unions, and contacts were made with members of Congress and other persons in public life, with special attention to the molders of public opinion. Not a stone was left unturned."[7]

AZEC's grassroots effort was enormously successful. Added to their mailing campaigns, rallies, and petitions was the threat that the Jews would stop supporting Democratic candidates with their votes and contributions. New York politicians were especially concerned and let Truman know it. Truman resented the pressure and it produced a backlash. He questioned whether the Zionist agenda was in America's best interests or offered the most satisfactory long-term solution for Palestine. He suspected that Silver's attacks on him were politically motivated. Silver's behavior also infuriated him. In the summer of 1946, a Zionist delegation came to see Truman to protest British arrests of Jewish leaders in Palestine. Silver confronted Truman and demanded that the president rein in the British. After Silver left, Abe Feinberg, a Jewish businessman who later became an important financier of Truman's 1948 campaign, came in to see him. He found the president "red in the face." Was anything wrong? Feinberg asked him. Truman answered, "Yes, damn it, the presidency is something to be respected, and that clown had the nerve to shake his finger in front of me…. I told him he'd never be welcome here again."[8] While Truman had sympathy for the Jewish survivors, it was incidents such as this one, as well as the denunciations of him from the Zionist movement, that led him to condemn those he called "extreme Zionists," to vent his rage in private against them, and to repeat his mantra that the Jews, like other groups, abused their power once they were on top. In the most recently discovered diary entry, he went so far as to compare them to Stalin and Hitler.

The president's negative reaction alarmed the Jewish Agency, whose leaders realized how important Truman's support was at a time when the State Department was doing everything in its power to derail the creation of the Jewish state. It "caused us serious concern about the outcome of our struggle," wrote Eliahu Epstein (later Elath), the Jewish Agency's representative in America, and led us to turn to our friends in the White House to "rectify … the situation."[9]

The men Epstein was pinning his hopes on were Jewish Americans who had themselves undergone profound changes in their views of Zionism. Judge

Samuel Rosenman, whom Truman retained along with David Niles from FDR's administration, summed up his own trajectory: "Before Hitler came to power I was an anti-Zionist, then after that I became a non-Zionist. At the end of the war, I became a full believer in the idea of political Zionism."[10] Epstein, who went on to become Israel's first ambassador to the United States, believed that although Rosenman and Niles never belonged to any Zionist organization, they became the people around Truman most dedicated to supporting the Zionist cause. When Truman refused to see Zionist leaders, Rosenman and Niles helped to counter the arguments and actions of opponents in the State Department as well as those of anti-Zionist Jews like Lessing Rosenwald who were getting an audience with the president. Rosenman had been especially helpful to Epstein when he first came to Washington from Palestine. He helped the newcomer understand the inner workings of the government, pointed out who was important, and how to act and how to approach them.[11]

The son of Russian Jewish immigrants, Rosenman had attended Columbia University Law School. He became FDR's counsel and chief speechwriter in 1928, when Roosevelt was running for the position of governor of New York. He continued in this role when FDR became president. As close as he was to Roosevelt, Rosenman thought it was inappropriate to lobby him about Jewish concerns. As the situation of Europe's Jews deteriorated during the war, however, Rosenman became bolder. He followed the example of Secretary of the Treasury Henry Morgenthau Jr., who confronted Roosevelt over the State Department's opposition to allowing Jewish refugees fleeing Hitler into the United States. Rosenman then became a major supporter of the creation of a War Refugee Board that he hoped would implement rescue. [12]

When Truman became president, he realized that Rosenman's two-decades-long relationship with Roosevelt would serve him well, and asked him to stay on in the same capacity. Truman was very conscious of the fact that he only held the job because of FDR's sudden death and that it was FDR's policies that had the nation's approval. The Oval Office had a picture of FDR on the wall, and Truman would glance at it and say to Rosenman, "I'm trying to do what he would like." Rosenman thought Truman looked to him for advice because "he knew that I knew what Roosevelt would have liked."[13]

When Truman turned to Rosenman for advice about the Jews and Palestine, the latter was reluctant to get involved because he didn't want to be in conflict with the State Department. However, since Truman had asked him and needed his help, Rosenman gave his honest opinion and soon became involved in the issue. Shortly after Truman became president, unknown correspondence between FDR and Saudi Arabia's King Ibn Saud surfaced. Saud's letter was an attack on Jewish claims in Palestine, and FDR assured him that he would "take no action … which might prove hostile to the Arab people" and that U.S. policy remained unchanged. Up to that point, the United States did not have much of a policy except to say that they would not support any changes in the basic situation in Palestine before consulting with the Arabs and the Jews.[14]

Truman showed the letters to Rosenman. Truman had been pressing British Prime Minister Clement Attlee for the admittance of 100,000 Jewish refugees to Palestine. Would this have any bearing on it? No, Rosenman advised, he did not think that admitting 100,000 Jews to Palestine meant there was a "change in the basic situation." As he read the Ibn Saud–FDR correspondence, Roosevelt had not made any promise beyond saying he would first consult with both Arab and Jewish leaders, "but that there was no intention on his part that he would have to obtain their consent before he took action."[15] Truman, he advised, should continue to pressure Attlee for the admission of 100,000 Jews to Palestine. Next, if he felt the need to, the president could call a conference of both Jewish and Arab leaders and formally consult with them, thereby fulfilling FDR's promise. After that, Rosenman told Truman, "you can take whatever action you wish."[16] Rosenman reminded Truman that while FDR's letter appeared to be pro-Arab, at other times Roosevelt had stated he favored Jewish immigration to Palestine and "even" the establishment of a Jewish commonwealth there. Rosenman said that Truman had to take into account that FDR's letter was written "a week before the President died and [covered an issue] which, I am sure, he [FDR] did not fully understand."[17]

When the British presented Truman with their terms of reference for the Anglo-American Committee, Truman asked Rosenman to look them over. "I think it is a complete run out on the Mandate," Rosenman told Truman. The terms of reference made no connection between the refugees and Palestine, a connection the British wanted to avoid. Truman then made certain that the option of Palestine as a destination for the refugees was formally put into the proposal.[18] The final version included the caveat that the committee would first look at "conditions in Palestine as they bear upon the problem of Jewish immigration," as well as carry out estimates "of those [Jews] who wish, or who will be impelled by their conditions, to migrate to Palestine…." Truman also took Rosenman's advice that he announce the Committee after the 6 November elections in New York, to prevent it from becoming a political football.[19] At Truman's request, Rosenman submitted a list of possible American candidates for the Committee. Two of them, Bartley Crum and James McDonald, became the Committee's strongest supporters of the Jewish position. Truman eventually appointed McDonald as America's first ambassador to Israel.

After Rosenman left the White House to enter private practice, he continued to be of service to the Zionist cause, acting as Truman's emissary to Chaim Weizmann. Perhaps most important was that Rosenman served as a mentor to Clark Clifford, who replaced him as Truman's special counsel in February 1946. Although some have claimed that Clifford's support for a Jewish state was solely calculated to win the Jewish vote for Truman, there was another dimension to Clifford's feelings on the subject. When Clifford arrived at the White House in 1945 as the assistant to Truman's naval aide Jake Vardaman, he knew little about the issues surrounding the Middle East or about tensions in Palestine between the British, the Arabs, and the Jews. Rosenman, noticing that Clifford had little to do, asked the young attorney if he wanted to work with him. During the time they spent together, Rosenman and Clifford discussed the situation of the Jews and their need for a homeland. "I learned a good deal from Judge Rosenman," Clifford later wrote, "….he felt strongly about it." Abe Feinberg, a major Democratic contributor who visited Truman in the White House, was surprised to find "a handsome WASP like Clifford to be so involved," but he was, and Feinberg was impressed by Clifford's empathy and understanding of the Jewish position.[20] Clifford wrote that, by the time Truman consulted with him on the issue, "I was sympathetic" and had become "an advocate of the Jewish State."[21]

Matthew Connelly, Truman's appointments secretary, had urged Truman to also retain David K. Niles. If Truman lost Niles, Connelly told him, "he would lose somebody who would be completely loyal to him," who backed him for nomination as vice president in 1944, and who could be invaluable working for Truman in the same job he had for FDR, as an adviser on minority groups, focusing mainly on the Jewish community and New York City politics. Niles, Connelly told Truman, "was a very bright political analyst. He was quiet, he was receptive, he was never out in front."[22]

Born in 1890, Niles grew up in Boston's rough North End, where his father was a tailor. Always a hard worker, Niles earned a place at the elite Boston Latin School, and upon graduation, got a job in the Information Office of the Department of Labor during World War I. Unable to afford college, Niles engaged in a process of self-education. He gravitated towards the Ford Hall Forum, a Boston institution that was a center of lectures and discussions for the city's intellectual community, eventually becoming its associate director. In that capacity, he made important political connections. Eventually, he came to Washington to work for the New Deal and became a personal assistant to Harry Hopkins, FDR's top aide.[23]

Niles had served FDR as a liaison with the Jews who were lobbying the president during the war on the difficult issues of rescue, refugees, and Palestine. He counseled them to put their faith in FDR, telling Bernard Joseph, a leader of the Jewish Agency, that FDR "shared the Zionist aims with regard to Palestine."[24] Roosevelt counted on Niles to advise him on which Jewish leaders he had to see and which ones he could put off without harming his political capital with Jewish constituents. He continued to take this role with Truman. As he explained to one of Truman's aides, "I envision my chief job to protect the President" from those who might "create some political damage."[25] Often, the political damage was coming from AZEC and Rabbi Silver, whom Niles did not like, as opposed to the more restrained and respectful approach that the Jewish Agency and the moderate Zionists took towards Truman. The difference between extreme and moderate Zionists was often one of style and behavior, not of the desired end result.

Truman put Niles in charge of all the information coming to the White House that had to do with the issue of Palestine and the Jews.[26] The president routinely asked for his advice, and Niles tried not to be out of step with Truman, whom he served as faithfully and loyally as he had Roosevelt. When the president wanted to limit his focus to the refugees, Niles made sure that was the issue addressed. He kept Truman informed on how his policies and directives were being carried out in the various departments of government, especially the State Department, whose officers consistently opposed the creation of a Jewish state.[27]

As the focus shifted from the refugees to finding a workable solution to the Palestine question, Niles advised Truman on the various plans put before him. Niles helped to move Truman away from taking decisions that would have harmed the possibility of creating a viable Jewish state. For a while, Truman seemed favorable towards the Morrison-Grady Plan, which was a British-inspired follow-up to the Anglo-America Committee's recommendations. Zionist critics rejected it as a plan that would have created a sham autonomy, depriving the Jewish state of access to the Dead Sea, the Galilee, and the Negev, and granting it only 1,500 square miles. Although Truman saw that plan as a way of finally getting the British to allow the immigration of the 100,000 refugees, Niles advised him to reject it, pointing out to him that he would be accused of giving up everything for this limited goal. Truman reluctantly rejected it, causing Secretary of State Byrnes, who supported it, to complain that "Niles and Sam Rosenman were chiefly responsible for the President's decision."[28]

Truman felt defeated over the failure of the Anglo-American Committee and the Morrison-Grady Plan. His best efforts to find a solution had gone nowhere. Jewish Agency leader Nahum Goldmann was in Paris attending a meeting of their executive committee when he received an urgent phone call from David Niles. Truman, Niles told him, was fed up with both the British and the American Zionists, and was "threatening to wash his hands of the whole matter." The only thing that would stop him was if the Jewish Agency came up with an alternative and realistic plan to substitute for Morrison-Grady.

Goldmann and other members of the Jewish Agency executive had been considering distancing themselves from the Zionists' Biltmore Resolution of 1943, which called for a Jewish state in the entire area of Palestine, and adopting the more realistic goal of partition. Unless they accepted partition, they reasoned, Jews were destined to be a minority in an Arab state. Wouldn't it be better to have a smaller state where they would be in control of their destiny? If Truman actually washed his hands of the Palestine issue, it would be, in Goldmann's eyes, "a worse catastrophe than an open state of war with England."[29]

After a few days of discussion, the Jewish Agency executive adopted a resolution stating that the Agency was "prepared to discuss a proposal for the establishment of a viable Jewish state in an *adequate* area of Palestine." That area would have to have full autonomy, including control over immigration.[30] The executive charged Goldmann with presenting their proposal. The first step was for him to get support for it from the various representatives of the American Jewish community, both Zionist and non-Zionist, and from the U.S. government. First, he met with Rabbi Silver and laid out the executive's plan. Silver, who resented Goldmann's interference in American Zionist affairs and was a supporter of the Biltmore Resolution, nonetheless agreed to go along with the majority resolution and not to interfere with his negotiations.

Goldmann met three times with Assistant Secretary of State Dean Acheson before he was able to convince him that partition was feasible and perhaps the only way out. Acheson thought he could support such a plan and advised him on how to proceed. He must convince David Niles, Secretary of the Treasury John W. Snyder, and Secretary of War John Patterson to support the partition plan. Goldmann knew that David Niles was very important to Truman and had been one of the moderate Zionists' "best and most loyal friends in Washington." However, he also believed that Niles "is not very much in favor of a Jewish State…. He helps us very much, but he never was ideologically a Zionist." It was difficult to sit down and talk to Niles during the day, so Goldmann went to see him at the hotel where he kept a room. According to Goldmann, after a two-hour talk, Niles was convinced that the Jewish Agency's new resolution was the only way out of the impasse.[31] Goldmann also persuaded Snyder and Patterson, as well as Judge Joseph Proskauer, the anti-Zionist head of the American Jewish Committee, to support the partition plan.[32]

Now that Goldmann had gotten the necessary parties to agree, it was decided that Niles and Acheson would present the partition plan to Truman with their endorsement. On 9 August 1946, Goldmann once again went to see Niles at his hotel room. "With tears in his eyes," Niles told him "that the President had accepted the plan without reservation and had instructed Dean Acheson to inform the British government."[33] Even though the British rejected it, this proposal was important because it led Jewish leaders in America and Palestine to reach a consensus supporting partition. It also marked a turning point in the evolution of Truman's view of the Palestine crisis. He had been unable to work out a solution with the British and so was just stating the facts when he made his famous Yom Kippur message in 1946, announcing that the Jewish Agency had agreed to the "creation of a viable Jewish state in control of [part] of Palestine," and that he now believed that "a solution along these lines would command the support of public opinion in the United States."[34]

As events unfolded and the realization of a Jewish state became a real possibility, Niles increasingly became an advocate. The moderate Zionists considered him to be their best friend in the White House. He gave them advice on how to approach the president, met with them in his office, and helped draft statements and letters. Truman was aware of his aide's emotional involvement in the issue and considered his advice accordingly.

When one mentions Truman's recognition of Israel to American Jews, they inevitably ask, "Didn't he have a Jewish business partner who had something to do with it?" Truman first met Eddie Jacobson when the fourteen-year-old stock boy for a Kansas City clothing store would bring the business's deposits to the Union National Bank, where the twenty-one-year-old Truman worked. They lost touch after Truman returned to the family farm in Grandview, only to meet up again in 1917, when Jacobson enlisted in the Missouri National Guard after the American entrance into World War I. It was fate that Truman would be first lieutenant of the battery to which Jacobson was assigned. The two set up an army canteen that was enormously successful. Truman wrote home to his girlfriend Bess Wallace, "I have a Jew in charge of the canteen by the name of Jacobson and he is a crackerjack."[35]

After serving in France, the two men returned home to an uncertain future. Pooling their savings, they opened a men's clothing store in downtown Kansas City, for which Truman did the bookkeeping and Jacobson the buying. At first the store was enormously successful and served as a meeting place for their old friends and army buddies, but the postwar depression of 1921 led to the business's failure. Truman went on to become a judge in the Jackson County

Court, while Jacobson went on the road as a salesman, eventually opening another store in Kansas City. The two remained close; some said they were almost like brothers.[36] That their relationship remained strong was surprising, given the fact that the same year they opened their store, Truman married Bess Wallace and lived with her in her mother's house. One of Mrs. Wallace's rules was that Jews were not welcome.

Jacobson had moved away from his parents' Orthodox Judaism and joined a Reform congregation, where he and his family faithfully attended Friday night services. After the Second World War, he joined B'nai B'rith, the Jewish fraternal organization, which had a non-Zionist position. Jacobson, described as a simple, modest man, had to leave school after the eighth grade to help support his family. He did not know very much about Jewish history or Zionism, but news of what was happening to the Jews in Europe made him acutely concerned for his people, with whom he felt a strong connection. Eddie Jacobson's education was about to begin, conducted in part by his friend and attorney A. J. Granoff, who held leadership positions within B'nai B'rith and had also been friendly with Truman in Kansas City.

As soon as Jewish leaders learned that one of Truman's good friends was Jewish, they sought out Jacobson's help, urging him to intercede with the president, first on the issue of the Jewish refugees, and then on supporting a Jewish state. Jacobson turned them down; he didn't want to be used to get to the president and he didn't want to bother Truman. But he changed his mind after several conversations with Reform Rabbi Arthur Lelyveld, whose job, according to his son, was to "stump from one major Jewish community to the next converting anti-Zionists and winning over those who had yet to commit themselves."[37] After several meetings with the persuasive rabbi, Jacobson agreed to take Lelyveld with him to see Truman.[38] The meeting took place on June 26, 1946. Lelyveld left with what he called "encouraging impressions." Truman seemed committed to gaining admission for the 100,000. But Lelyveld worried that Truman appeared to be too impressed with threats coming from the Arab League, and was repeating the State Department's arguments that Arab guerrilla warfare would interfere with access to oil supply lines.[39]

Jacobson visited Truman in the White House at least twenty-four times, thirteen of them off the record.[40] His friend Abe Granoff accompanied him about seven of those times. According to Granoff, Truman was always happy to see his old friends and would grill them about their wives and children and would want to know every detail about how Eddie's business was doing. Truman acted the same way towards them as he did back home in Missouri, but his friends often felt nervous, well aware that they were not just visiting their old friend and poker partner, but the president of the United States. The men considered themselves to be non-Zionists. "To be a Zionist in the days we started talking to the President," recalled Granoff, "was like waving a red flag in front of him, because they [the AZEC] abused him terribly, frightfully. They tried to contact us all the time, but we wouldn't speak to them."[41]

However, the difference in the positions of the non-Zionists and the Zionists practically disappeared after the United Nations General Assembly, on 29 November 1947, approved a plan for partition, dividing Palestine into three entities: a Jewish state, an Arab state, and an international zone around Jerusalem. Soon after, the British announced that they would be pulling out of Palestine on 15 May, whereupon the Jewish leaders in Palestine declared that they would then announce the founding of their state. Although the United States was officially on record as supporting partition, the State Department, which had influence over the American delegates to the United Nations, still opposed it. Supporters of partition suspected that they were engineering a double-cross at the UN. Since Truman was refusing to see any of the American "extreme Zionist" leaders, they thought it urgent that Chaim Weizmann go to see the president. Nahum Goldmann observed that "Weizmann was an overwhelming figure. Anyone who encountered him fell under his spell."[42] This was true for Lord Balfour in 1917 and it was true for Truman.

Weizmann had been called on before to meet with Truman, when the State Department was trying to switch the Negev from the Jewish to the Arab portion specified in the partition plan. Weizmann, who was a noted chemist, painted a picture for Truman that appealed to him as the farmer he had once been. By using desalted water, the Jews would make the desert bloom. Their experiments with desalination were already producing carrots, bananas, and potatoes in areas where nothing had grown for hundreds of years. If taken from the Jews, it would remain a desert. Aqaba, too, was crucial, Weizmann told the president. It was now a useless bay that had to be dredged, deepened, and made into a waterway that could accommodate large ships. If it was part of a Jewish state, Weizmann told Truman, "it would make a real contribution to trade and commerce by opening up a new route." It would be a parallel highway to the Suez Canal, shortening the route from Europe to India by a day or more. Truman agreed that the Negev should remain part of the Jewish state. "I was extremely happy," Weizmann later wrote. Truman then "promised that he would communicate [that] at once with the American delegation at Lake Success."[43] Truman kept his word.

But now, Truman would not even see Weizmann. The situation was dire.

David Niles was away due to illness and couldn't keep Truman apprised of the reactions of the Jewish community or alert him to the rumors of an impending State Department plan to reverse his policy. In mid-February of 1948, Weizmann, who at that time held no official position in the Zionist movement, was in London, on his way back home to Rehovoth, when he received a call from his protégé at the Jewish Agency, Aubrey Eban, urging him to return to the United States and see Truman. Weizmann then wrote Truman asking for an audience in Washington before Truman left for a scheduled vacation in Key West. Truman's appointments secretary, Matt Connelly, responded that the president's calendar was full.[44]

Frank Goldman, B'nai B'rith's national president, called Jacobson in the middle of the night and told him that Truman was refusing to see any of the New York City political leaders who had been imploring him to see Weizmann. Truman apparently was angry "at leading American Zionists who denounced him for refusing to send American troops and supplies to fight the Arabs opposing the partition plan" and they were afraid that the president was washing his hands of the whole matter and was going to let the UN decide what should be done. Goldman wanted Jacobson to immediately get on a plane and see Truman before he left for Key West. Jacobson was their last hope.[45]

Jacobson couldn't make the arrangements, but sent a telegram to Connelly asking him to show it to the president immediately. "I know that you have very excellent reasons for not wanting to see Dr. Weizmann," Jacobson wrote. He understood more than anyone else the pressure on the president. "But as you once told me," he wrote, "this gentleman is the greatest statesman and finest leader that my people have. He is very old and heartbroken that he could not get to see you." Noting that he had not asked Truman for "favors during all our years of friendship," he now wrote that I "am begging of you to see Dr. Weizmann.... I can assure you I would not plead to you for any other of our leaders."[46]

Truman wrote back that there was nothing Weizmann could possibly say that he did not already know. Truman confessed that Palestine "has been a headache to me for two and a half years. The Jews are so emotional, and the Arabs so difficult...that it is almost impossible to get anything done." The British, moreover, were not cooperating, while "the Zionists...expected a big stick approach on our part." He had concluded that "the situation is not solvable as presently set up."[47]

On 12 March, paying his own way as always, Jacobson flew to the capital from Kansas City. He had no appointment at the White House, but took his chances that Truman would see him. At the entrance to the Oval Office, he encountered Connelly, who "advised and urged and begged" him not to discuss Palestine with the president. Jacobson told Connelly, "That's what I came to Washington for, and…I was determined to discuss this very subject with the President."[48]

Entering the Oval Office, Jacobson soon brought up Palestine. Truman "immediately became tense in appearance," Jacobson wrote, "…and very bitter in the words he was throwing my way." Jacobson was stunned, since he had never "talked to me in this manner." Truman made it clear he did not want to talk about Palestine at all. But Jacobson summoned his courage and argued "from every possible angle." Truman complained about how disrespectful and mean certain Jewish leaders had been to him, obviously thinking of Rabbi Silver. Next, Truman let out a string of vituperative statements of the kind he made in private at moments of great frustration. He had never talked that way or even raised his voice to his old friend, who was shocked. "At that moment," Jacobson thought, Truman came "as close to being an anti-Semite as a man could possibly be." As for himself, he was upset that some American Jewish leaders were responsible for Truman's harsh feelings.

Jacobson was about out of arguments, when he looked at the statue Truman kept in his office of his favorite president, Andrew Jackson. He had thought about making some connection between Weizmann and Jackson that might convince Truman. According to Aubrey Eban, Jacobson had called to ask for his advice about trying that line of argument. Eban told him that although "no two human beings had ever walked on the face of the earth with fewer common attributes than Chaim Weizmann and Andrew Jackson," he should go ahead and try it.[49] So he did. He told Truman that just as he (Truman) had a hero in Andrew Jackson, so he (Jacobson) had a personal hero in Chaim Weizmann, whom he considered "the greatest Jew who ever lived." He emphasized that Truman himself considered Weizmann a gentleman and great statesman. He had traveled thousands of miles in ill health to see Truman. "Now you refuse to see him because you were insulted by some of our American Jewish leaders," knowing that Weizmann had nothing to do with their tactics. "It doesn't sound like you, Harry."

Truman began to drum on his desk with his fingers. He "turned around while still sitting in his swivel chair and started looking out the window.… Jacobson knew the sign that Truman was changing his mind." Seconds that seemed like many minutes passed between the two men in silence. Truman suddenly swiveled around and faced Jacobson, "looked me straight in the eyes and then said the most endearing words I had ever heard from his lips."

"You win, you baldheaded son of a bitch. I will see him. Tell Matt to arrange this meeting as soon as possible after I return from New York on March 17."

At that moment, Connelly entered the room. Truman told him immediately to schedule in Weizmann. It was to be an off-the-record meeting, the president said, and the press and public were not to know anything about it. Rushing to the Statler Hotel, Jacobson met Frank Goldman and Maurice Bisgyer of B'nai B'rith, who were anxiously waiting to hear Truman's decision. Jacobson was so nervous and excited he first rushed to the bar and guzzled down two double bourbons, an unprecedented act for him. The three men then made their arrangements to go to New York, where Jacobson would meet Weizmann for the first time. Jacobson had made some kind of breakthrough with Truman that no one else had been able to do. Perhaps Truman had been persuaded by his arguments or maybe he just couldn't say no to his friend who had asked for so little and who was so passionate about his request.

The critical meeting of Truman and Weizmann took place on 18 March. Weizmann talked to Truman about the Jewish plans for the economic development of Palestine and the need to have land for future Jewish immigrants. He again emphasized the importance of the Negev. Truman told him he wanted to see "justice done without bloodshed." Weizmann told his wife upon returning to his hotel room that he had talked with Truman about lifting the embargo on arms sales, support for partition, and free immigration to Palestine. On the point they were most concerned about—partition—Truman told him that he fully supported it.[50]

The next day, the State Department launched its plan to reverse the United States position on partition before 15 May. Ambassador Warren Austin told the UN Security Council that because of continued violence in Palestine, the United States was now supporting a temporary trusteeship. Although Truman had been warned by Clifford and others that this would happen, it hit him like a bombshell. What really infuriated him, he told Clifford, was that yesterday he had "assured Chaim Weizmann that we were for partition and would stick to it. He must think I'm a plain liar."[51] Soon after, Truman asked Sam Rosenman to see Weizmann and explain to him what had happened. Rosenman reported that he found Weizmann enjoying a card game, philosophical, and confident that Truman would do the right thing. Appreciative of his reaction, Truman told Rosenman that in the future, he would only talk to Weizmann if the Zionists wanted to contact him.[52]

On 12 April, Jacobson visited Truman in the Oval Office and heard from "his friend's own lips" what happened at his meeting with Weizmann and how shocked he was to find one day later how Warren Austin betrayed him. Then, Jacobson said, Truman strongly reaffirmed the promises regarding partition that he had made to him and to Weizmann and gave him permission to tell Dr. Weizmann so. Jacobson now brought up the question of recognition with Truman. According to Jacobson, "to this he agreed with a whole heart."[53] Eleven days later, this message was reinforced by Truman when he told Sam Rosenman "I have Dr. Weizmann on my conscience." He wanted Rosenman to tell Weizmann that he planned to "recognize the Jewish State as soon as it was proclaimed."[54] The only thing that could interfere with that step was if the State Department's proposals passed at the United Nations, which did not happen.

When Truman announced on 8 March his intention to run for president in the 1948 election, he still had not completely made up his mind concerning what to do about Palestine. What made him finally decide? Weizmann's visits had reinforced his belief that the Jews, unlike the Arabs, would develop Palestine and make the desert bloom once again. They planned to establish a democratic form of government, which Truman hoped would serve as a model for the Middle East. Truman believed in progress, but beyond that, Palestine was a special place for him. It was the Holy Land. Although religion never came up in any official documents, it served as a backdrop. Truman was raised as a Baptist and was well versed in the Bible. He shared his thoughts with Clifford about biblical prophecies concerning the Jews' return to Zion in the Old Testament, which gave a certain stamp of approval from a higher order to his decision. Clifford, who considered himself an amateur Bible student, recalled exchanging passages with the president on the subject. One of Truman's favorites, which he often quoted, was from Deuteronomy: "Behold, I have given up the land before you. Go in and take possession of the land to which the Lord has sworn unto your fathers, to Abraham, to Isaac, and to Jacob." Others were from Genesis, which referred to "an everlasting possession."[55]

Similar memories came from Alfred Lilienthal, an anti-Zionist serving during the Truman administration in the State Department, and as a consultant to the American delegation to the UN during its founding conference. Truman, he wrote, "was a biblical fundamentalist who constantly pointed to these words of the Old Testament," citing the same passage from Deuteronomy to which Clifford had alluded.[56] Truman's hopes for Israel and the Middle East were on his mind when he gave his Farewell Address as president on 15 January 1953, in which he wished that "the Tigris and the Euphrates Valley can be made to bloom as it did in the time of Babylon and Nineveh. Israel can be made into the country of milk and honey, as it was in the time of Joshua."[57]

But religion was not uppermost in Truman's mind as 15 May 1948 approached. In the White House, Truman was surrounded by aides who favored partition and recognition either because they believed in the creation of a Jewish state or they believed that Truman would need the support of the Jews to win the presidential election. For most, it seemed to be a mixture of the two. Truman's White House advisers now made a concerted effort to present Truman with arguments to counter those he was hearing from the State Department. In March, Clark Clifford retained the help of attorney Max Lowenthal, an old associate of Truman's from his days as a senator on the Wheeler Subcommittee. Lowenthal had brought Truman along to the famous teas held by Justice Brandeis and had been instrumental in gaining labor's support for Truman's vice-presidential candidacy at the 1944 convention. Born in Minneapolis in 1888, Lowenthal went on to get his law degree at Harvard. After graduating, he worked with Felix Frankfurter on labor cases and on the War Labor Board during World War I. Frankfurter found his young protégé to be a "very sensitive fellow, particularly responsive to cruelty and hardship, and a very fine disciplined brain."[58] Now Clifford enlisted him to research and draft a paper critiquing the positions enunciated by the State Department in the previous few months against partition, and making a case for partition.[59]

Next, Clifford composed another memo addressing Truman's concerns. Palestine, he advised Truman, should not be considered as a Jewish issue, but should be considered from the standpoint of "what is best for the United States of America." Addressing Truman's sensitivity to charges that he was acting out of political motives, Clifford wrote:

> In advising as to what is best for America, [you] must in no sense be influenced by the election this fall. I know only too well that you would not hesitate to follow a course of action that makes certain the defeat of the Democratic Party if you thought such action were best for America.

Then Clifford laid out the course of action that would be best for America. The State Department's arguments were "completely fallacious," he wrote, while Truman's support of partition was "completely in harmony with the policy of the United States." If he turned against it, Truman would be departing from already established and accepted policy, which would make him "justifiably subject to criticism." Next, Clifford assured Truman that partition offered the best hope to avoid war and to offer a permanent solution. To drift and delay, as others advocated, would lead to the very military involvement they claimed they wanted to avoid.

Turning to the new Cold War, Clifford argued that support of partition was the only course that would strengthen the American position vis-à-vis the Soviet Union, since the Soviets had unexpectedly decided to also support it. There was concern in the State Department that Israel might become a zone of Soviet influence. Why boost their influence with the new Jewish state, he argued, since opposing partition would do just that? By constantly shifting their position, our foreign policy was failing, and Clifford warned that many Americans feared the collapse of the UN, a force they had hoped would be a forerunner of world peace. Much worse, they felt that their own nation was "aiding and abetting in the disintegration of the United Nations."

To bolster confidence and to maintain an anti-Soviet alliance, it was necessary for America's own "selfish interests" to support the UN resolution on Palestine. Clifford reminded Truman, "We 'crossed the Rubicon' on this matter when the partition resolution was adopted…largely at your insistence." To back away would lead other nations never to trust America's commitments. As for those who argued that the U.S. would lose oil because the Arabs would not sell their supply to America, he answered that "the Arab states must have oil royalties or go broke." The Saudis got 90 percent of their oil revenue from America, and they would not jeopardize that. "Their need of the United States is greater than our need of them."[60]

As 15 May drew closer, Lowenthal researched and drafted at least six more reports for Clifford. In a 9 May memorandum, Lowenthal argued that the Jews had on their own, in effect, made partition a reality. Not only did the Jews militarily control the Jewish part of Palestine, but they maintained and ran what was in effect a government. Partition was a reality; the only question was whether it could be reversed. That would be impossible. The bottom line was that "it is unrealistic to believe that the Jews of Palestine could be persuaded to relinquish the State which they achieved largely through their own efforts."[61] Lowenthal advised that the president issue an early statement of his intention to recognize the new Jewish state in Palestine as soon as it came into existence. Such an announcement could force the Arabs to accept what was inevitable, since they would note the American support. If Truman did not act, the Soviet Union certainly would, and any similar action by the United States would "seem begrudging, no matter how well-intentioned," and would also amount to a "diplomatic defeat."

Truman's recognition would also have the effect of defusing it as a political issue at home, since the Republicans were certain to push hard on its behalf. To accept the reality and recognize the Jewish state would mean, Lowenthal argued, that "we will not be used by Arab or Republican politicians, we will help to retrieve the prestige of the UN and U.S., and we will cease to subject President Truman to unjust and unjustified losses and sacrifices." The moment to act had come, Lowenthal argued. The opportunity for Truman "is fast vanishing." If the U.S. continued to withhold recognition and seek to "satisfy the *amour propre* of a few State Department officials," he wrote, "the opportunity to undo the damage to the President may fade out."

David Niles and Appointments Secretary Matt Connelly went to Truman and presented their arguments for why they thought he should recognize Israel right away. Connelly said he took the position he did for two reasons: "One, it was humanitarian, and two, it was good politics. I raised the question with Mr. Truman, 'How many Arab votes are there in the United States? Where does the Democratic Party get its financing from?' The answer was apparent."[62]

Truman asked Clifford to prepare a presentation for an important meeting with the State Department on 12 May. He was to make the case that a statement should be issued by the president saying that he intended to recognize the Jewish state when statehood was announced. Clifford asked Niles and Lowenthal to supply him with arguments. Truman revered his popular secretary of state, George C. Marshall, and, facing a tough election in the fall, could not afford to lose him over the issue. After a heated discussion, the State Department's view prevailed when they argued that there was no precedent for the United States government to issue recognition to a government in advance of their making an application for it. However, through eleventh-hour negotiations, Clifford got Marshall to at least agree not to issue any public opposition to Truman's recognition when the State of Israel was actually declared, clearing an important obstacle to Truman's actions on 14 May.

At a press conference on 13 May, when asked what he intended to do the next day, the president enigmatically said he would "cross that bridge when I get to it." When he saw Niles there, he told him that he was sorry he had to decide "against you fellows yesterday." Truman thought Marshall and his undersecretary of state, Robert Lovett, meant well, "but they follow their associates," and he told Niles that he didn't give any credence to their arguments that the Jewish state would be infiltrated by Communists.

Truman had sworn Weizmann to secrecy about his plan to recognize the Jewish state the next day, and he was keeping his intentions close to his vest. Apparently he hadn't even confided in Lowenthal or Niles. Niles now urged him to recognize the Jewish state before the Soviets or any of their satellites did. "That is right," Truman replied. "The Western recognition should precede the Soviet bloc's … so as to give it the right slant from the beginning." Niles also emphasized that many mass rallies were scheduled in America to honor the proclamation, and that he and Max Lowenthal "were trying to prevent any adverse references to him" that might occur if he did not offer U.S. recognition. But they were sure Truman "would work out this whole affair satisfactorily." Someday, Truman replied, he would let the world know how much he appreciated what they had been doing.[63]

When Truman announced the U.S. recognition of Israel at 6:11 p.m. on the evening of May 14, he turned to one of his aides and said, speaking of Chaim Weizmann, "The old Doctor will believe me now."[64] He then called David Niles. Truman wanted him to know that he had just announced recognition. "You're the first person I called," he said, "because I knew how much this would mean to you."[65]

All of these Jewish contacts of Truman had played a major role in the events leading to his recognition of Israel. His friend Eddie Jacobson had become an important intermediary between the Zionist movement and the president. Writing to Jacobson in 1952, Vera Weizmann told him, "Only the most intimate friends knew the extraordinary role that was played by you in swinging the scale in our favor when the future looked so precarious and ambiguous."[66]

David Niles, the Jewish Agency's "friend in Washington," became a devoted supporter of a Jewish state and helped take Truman on that same road. As Chaim Weizmann wrote him in 1949, although it might be "too soon to evaluate" his role in Israel's history, he knew that Niles had "played no insignificant part in the making of this history." Weizmann was certain that Niles had "good reason to be proud" that he had helped "bring about a proper understanding of the ideals of our cause in high places in Washington."[67] When Niles handed Truman his letter of resignation due to ill health in 1951, Truman wrote to him, "You have been a tower of strength to me during the past six years and I can't tell you how very much I appreciate it."[68]

Max Lowenthal, like David Niles, preferred to keep a low profile, but Truman wanted him to step forward and take credit for being a "benefactor to the State of Israel." In 1952, Truman wrote to Lowenthal that although the "Israelites have placed me on a pedestal alongside of Moses," he didn't know anyone who had "done more for Israel than you have." Truman reminded Lowenthal that his advice had been crucial and that he was the one Truman talked to when they were trying to work out recognition.[69]

If Samuel Rosenman was criticized for not doing enough for the Jews during World War II, he made up for it by his contributions to the Zionist cause during

Truman's administration. Eliahu Elath was so appreciative that in 1976 he wrote for an Israeli journal his own account of the importance of Rosenman's role in Israel's creation. With that article, Rosenman's contributions were preserved for history.

Without the effort of these four men, the recognition of Israel would not have been a certainty. At this conference, it is time to acknowledge the major influence they had on Harry S. Truman.

Notes

1. Jewish Agency, Memorandum, "To the Political Dept., Note on the New President of the United States," reprinted in Fink, *America and Palestine,* 153.
2. *New York Times,* "Congressmen Plan to See More Camps," 27 April 1945, p.3.
3. CBS News, "The Conflicts of Harry S. Truman: At War With the Experts," 1964, HSTL Film Collection.
4. Truman, *Harry S. Truman,* 416–19.
5. Quoted in Adler, *Roots in a Moving Stream,* 201.
6. Adler, *Roots in a Moving Stream,* 128. See also Grose, *Israel in the Mind of America,* 166–67.
7. Neumann, *In the Arena,* 214.
8. Truman, quoted in Pace, "Abraham Feinberg, Philanthropist for Israel."
9. Elath, "Harry S. Truman."
10. Elath, "Samuel Irving Rosenman and His Contribution before the Establishment of Israel."
11. Elath, "Samuel Irving Rosenman and His Contribution before the Establishment of Israel."
12. Rosen, *Saving the Jews,* 29.
13. Rosenman, Interview, 15 October 1968.
14. The letters were published verbatim in *The New York Times,* 19 October 1945, p. 4.
15. Samuel I. Rosenman, "Memorandum for the President," 17 October 1945, Harry S. Truman Subject File, Box 160, HSTL; also copied in Samuel I. Rosenman Papers, Box 4, HSTL.
16. Samuel I. Rosenman, "Memorandum for the President," 17 October 1945, Harry S. Truman Subject File, Box 160, HSTL; also copied in Samuel I. Rosenman Papers, Box 4, HSTL.
17. Rosenman "Memorandum," 18 October 1945, Samuel I. Rosenman Papers, Box 4, HSTL.
18. Samuel Rosenman, "Memo for the President," 17 October 1945, Subject File, Box 160, HSTL.
19. Byrnes to Halifax, 23 October 1945, in U.S. Dept. of State, *Foreign Relations, 1945,* 8:785–86.
20. Feinberg, interview, 23 August 1973.
21. Clifford, interview, 4 May 1988.
22. Connelly, interview, 21 August 1968.
23. Our discussion is based on Grose, *Israel in the Mind of America,* 219; Donovan, *Conflict and Crisis,* 316; and Cohen, "The United Nations in Its Twentieth Year."
24. Minutes of conversation with David Niles by Bernard Joseph, 6 December 1944, Confidential memo #1386, CZA. Another less complete memo of the same conversation appears in a short summary dated 27 November 1944, #1386, CZA.
25. Quoted in Ganin, *American Jewry and Israel, 1945–1948,* 24.
26. Elath, "Samuel Irving Rosenman and His Contribution before the Establishment of Israel."
27. Truman to Benjamin V. Cohen, 1965, read by Cohen in his speech, "The United Nations

in Its Twentieth Year."

28. Forrestal Diary, 3 December 1947, in Millis, *Forrestal Diaries,* 347.

29. Nahum Goldmann, Address to Hadassah National Board, 28 October 1946, Jewish Agency files, 1924–1945, Box 6, AJHS, New York City.

30. Goldmann, *Autobiography,* 131–32. Also see resolution adopted at meeting of the Executive of the Jewish Agency in Paris, 5 August 1946, CZA L35/121.

31. Nahum Goldmann, Address to Hadassah National Board, 28 October 1946, Jewish Agency files, 1924–1945, Box 6, AJHS, New York City.

32. Nahum Goldmann to Asst. Secretary of the Treasury Ed Foley, 8 August 1946, John W. Snyder Papers, Box 22, HSTL.

33. Goldmann, *Autobiography,* 235.

34. Statement by the President, 4 October 1946, David Niles Papers, quoted in Henry L. Shapiro to Chairmen of Local Emergency Committees and AZEC, 7 October 1946, Box 42, AJHS Papers, Box 33, HSTL.

35. Truman to Bess Wallace, 28 October 1917, in Ferrell, *Dear Bess,* 233.

36. Granoff, interviews, 9 April and 18 August 1969.

37. Lelyveld, *Omaha Blues,* 61, 75.

38. Adler, *Roots in a Moving Stream,* 204.

39. Lelyveld's report is reprinted in Ganin, *Truman, American Jewry and Israel,* 74–75; and Lelyveld to Silver, 1 July 1946, AZEC Papers.

40. Appointments files, HSTL; and Fellman, "An American Friendship."

41. Granoff, interviews, 9 April and 27 August 1969.

42. Goldmann, *Autobiography,* 109.

43. Weizmann, *Trial and Error,* 458–59. See also Donovan, *Conflict and Crisis,* 327.

44. Weizmann to Truman, 10 February 1948; Memo from Matt Connelly to Weizmann on behalf of President Truman, 12 February 1948, Box 10, Max Lowenthal Papers, University of Minnesota, Minneapolis.

45. *Kansas City Times,* "Zionist Leaders Turned to Kansas Citian," 13 May 1965; and Jacobson, "Two Presidents and a Haberdasher—1948."

46. Jacobson to Truman, 18 February 1948, Jacobson Papers, HSTL.

47. Truman to Jacobson, 27 February 1948, Jacobson Papers, HSTL.

48. Jacobson to Josef Cohn, 27 March 1952, A. J. Granoff Papers, Box 2, HSTL; and Jacobson, "Two Presidents and a Haberdasher—1948." The following account of their meeting is from these sources as well.

49. Eban, *Personal Witness,* 34.

50. Truman, *Years of Trial and Hope,* 189–90; and Weizmann, *The Impossible Takes Longer,* 228–29.

51. "Clifford Sets the Record Straight" [reprint of Clifford's talk at the 1976 annual meeting of the American Historical Association and the American Jewish Historical Society, "Factors Influencing President Truman's Decision to Support Partition and Recognize the State of Israel"] *Near East Report* 29 (Dec. 1976); and Clifford, interview, 26 October 1949. Clifford has Truman using a much more colorful word than "liar" in the latter version.

52. Elath, "Samuel Irving Rosenman and His Contribution before the Establishment of Israel."

53. Jacobson to Josef Cohn, 27 March 1952, p. 11, A. J. Granoff Papers, Box 2, HSTL.

54. Weizmann, *The Impossible Takes Longer,* 231.

55. Clifford, interview, 4 May 1988.

56. Lilienthal, "Remembering General George Marshall's Clash with Clark Clifford over Premature Recognition of Israel."

57. Elath, "Harry S. Truman—The Man and the Statesman," First Annual Harry S. Truman Lecture, 18 May 1977, Hebrew University of Jerusalem, Harry S. Truman Research Institute.
58. Frankfurter, *Felix Frankfurter Reminisces*, 136–37.
59. Cohen, *Truman and Israel*, 189.
60. Memorandum by Clifford to Truman, 8 March 1948, in U.S. Department of State, *Foreign Relations, 1948*, 5:690–96.
61. Lowenthal statement, 9 May 1948, Clark Clifford Papers, Box 13, HSTL. The discussion of Lowenthal's views is taken entirely from this memorandum.
62. Connelly, interview, 21 August 1968.
63. Max Lowenthal, Diary entry of 12 May 1948, Max Lowenthal Papers, Box 10, University of Minnesota, Minneapolis.
64. Weizmann, *The Impossible Takes Longer*, 234.
65. Sacher, "David K. Niles and United States Policy," 1.
66. Vera Weizmann to Jacobson, December 1952, Eddie Jacobson Papers, HSTL.
67. Weizmann to Niles, 20 February 1949, Chaim Weizmann Papers, Weizmann Institute of Science, Rehovot, Israel.
68. Truman to Niles, 17 May 1951, President's Secretary's File, HSTL.
69. Truman to Lowenthal, 23 April 1962, Post-Presidential Papers, HSTL. See Cohen, *Truman and Israel*, for a lengthy discussion of Lowenthal's role.

Works Cited

Adler, Frank J. *Roots in a Moving Stream: The Centennial History of Congregation B'nai Jehudah of Kansas City, 1870–1970*. Kansas City, MO: Congregation B'nai Jehudah, 1972.

CBS News. "The Conflicts of Harry S. Truman: At War with the Experts," 1964. HSTL Film Collection.

Clifford, Clark M. Interview by Jonathan Daniels, 26 October 1949. Transcript, Jonathan Daniels Papers, HSTL.

———. Interview by Richard Holbrooke and Brian Van Den Mark, 4 May 1988. Transcript, Holbrooke Papers, HSTL.

"Clifford Sets the Record Straight." Talk before the American Jewish Historical Society and the American Historical Association." *Near East Report* 20 (29 Dec. 1976).

Cohen, Benjamin V. "The United Nations in Its Twentieth Year." David Niles Memorial Lecture, Hebrew University, Harry S. Truman Research Institute for the Advancement of Peace, 27 April 1945. Copy in Loy W. Henderson Papers, Library of Congress, Washington, DC.

Cohen, Michael J. *Truman and Israel*. Berkeley: University of California Press, 1990.

Connelly, Matthew J. Interview by Jerry N. Hess, 21 August 1968, New York City. Transcript, Oral History Interviews, HSTL.

Donovan, Robert. *Conflict and Crisis: The Presidency of Harry S. Truman, 1945–1948*. New York: Norton, 1977.

Eban, Abba. *Personal Witness*. New York: G. P. Putnam's Sons, 1992.

Elath, Eliahu. "Harry S. Truman—The Man and the Statesman," First Annual Harry S. Truman Lecture, Hebrew University of Jerusalem, Harry S. Truman Research Institute for the Advancement of Peace, 18 May 1977.

———. "Samuel Irving Rosenman and His Contribution before the Establishment of Israel." [In Hebrew, translated by Tuvia Friling.] *Molad* 7, no. 37–38 (Spring 1976): 448–54.

Feinberg, Abraham. Interview by Richard D. McKinzie, 23 August 1973, New York City.

Transcript, Oral History Interviews, HSTL.

Fellman, Daniel J. "An American Friendship: A Critical Examination of the Life of Eddie Jacobson and His Relationship with President Harry S. Truman." PhD diss., Hebrew Union College, Jewish Institute of Religion, March 2005.

Ferrell, Robert H., ed. *Dear Bess: The Letters of Harry Truman to Bess Truman, 1910–1959.* New York: Norton, 1983.

Fink, Reuben. *America and Palestine: The Attitude of Official America and of the American People Toward the Rebuilding of Palestine as a Free and Democratic Jewish Commonwealth.* New York: American Zionist Emergency Council, 1944.

Frankfurter, Felix. *Felix Frankfurter Reminisces.* New York: Reynal, 1960.

Ganin, Zvi. *American Jewry and Israel, 1945–1948.* New York: Holmes and Meier, 1979.

Goldmann, Nahum. *The Autobiography of Nahum Goldmann: Sixty Years of Jewish Life.* New York: Holt, Rinehart, and Winston, 1969.

Granoff, A. J. Interview by J. R. Fuchs, 9 April and 27 August 1969. Transcript, Oral History Interviews, HSTL.

Grose, Peter. *Israel in the Mind of America.* New York: Knopf, 1983.

Jacobson, Eddie. "Two Presidents and a Haberdasher—1948." *American Jewish Archives Journal* 20 (April 1968): 3–15.

Kansas City Times, "Zionist Leaders Turned to Kansas Citian," 13 May 1965.

Lelyveld, Joseph. *Omaha Blues: A Memory Loop.* New York: Farrar, Straus and Giroux, 2005.

Lilienthal, Alfred M. "Remembering General George Marshall's Clash with Clark Clifford over Premature Recognition of Israel." *Washington Report on Middle East Affairs* 18, no. 4 (June 1999): 49–50.

Millis, Walter, ed. *The Forrestal Diaries.* New York: Viking Press, 1953.

Neumann, Emanuel. *In the Arena: An Autobiographical Memoir.* New York: Herzl Press, 1976.

New York Times, "Congressmen Plan to See More Camps," 27 April 1945, p. 3.

Pace, Eric. "Abraham Feinberg, Philanthropist for Israel." *New York Times,* Obituaries, 7 December 1998, B10.

Rosen, Robert N. *Saving the Jews: Franklin D. Roosevelt and the Holocaust.* New York: Thunder's Mouth Press, 2006.

Rosenman, Judge Samuel I. Interview by Jerry N. Ness, 15 October 1968, New York City. Transcript, Oral History Interviews, HSTL.

Sacher, David Bernard. "David K. Niles and United States Policy." Senior honors thesis, Harvard University, 1959.

Truman, Harry S. *Years of Trial and Hope.* Garden City, NY: Doubleday, 1956.

Truman, Margaret. *Harry S. Truman.* New York: Morrow, 1972.

U.S. State Department. *Foreign Relations of the United States, 1945.* Vol. 8, *The Near East and Africa.* Washington, DC: Government Printing Office, 1969.

Weizmann, Chaim. *The Letters and Papers of Chaim Weizmann,* edited by Leonard Stein. 23 vols. London: Oxford University Press, 1968–.

———. *Trial and Error: The Autobiography of Chaim Weizmann.* New York: Harper, 1949.

Weizmann, Vera. *The Impossible Takes Longer.* New York: Harper & Row, 1967.

Archives

AJHS   American Jewish Historical Society, New York, USA
AZEC   American Zionist Emergency Council, in Central Zionist Archives, Jerusalem
CZA   Central Zionist Archives, Jerusalem, Israel
HSTL   Harry S. Truman Library and Museum, Independence, Missouri, USA

Truman's Recognition of Israel
The Domestic Factor

Michael J. Cohen

Pᴿᴇsɪᴅᴇɴᴛ Hᴀʀʀʏ S. Tʀᴜᴍᴀɴ's sᴜᴘᴘᴏʀᴛ for Zionism—his prompt recognition of Israel just eleven minutes after Ben-Gurion's declaration of its independence—presents something of a paradox. Truman was a product of the nineteenth-century American Midwest, and as such, was something of a racist in his views, on the record as having expressed, albeit in private, anti-Semitic sentiments. However, due to the unique political situation that existed in the early post–World War II years—the Democrats' and Truman's own personal dependence on the Jewish vote and on Jewish donations—Truman was virtually coerced by his political advisers into supporting a cause that, at least until spring 1948, his own instincts inclined him to oppose.

Racial Prejudice and Anti-Semitism

Harry S. Truman was born in 1874 in the small, rural town of Independence, Missouri. His attitude to race, as revealed, for instance, in his letters to his fiancée (later his wife) Bess Wallace, have been attributed to "his family's Southern roots and prevailing views in turn-of-the-century Independence, Missouri." As a young man, Truman struggled to eke out a living as a farmer and, as was common in Missouri, he routinely spoke derogatorily of "blacks [always referred to in private as niggers], Jews, and Orientals."[1]

The young Truman developed an antipathy to foreign immigrants. He resented having to compete in the land market with nonnative Americans, whom he referred to as "bohunks" (a derogatory term for eastern and southeastern Europeans) and "Rooshans" (Russians).[2] In June 1911, Truman, then aged twenty-seven, in his letter proposing marriage to Bess, chose to confess his racist views to his wife-to-be:

> Uncle Will says that the Lord made a white man from dust, a nigger from
> mud, then he threw up what was left and it came down a Chinaman. He
> does hate Chinese and Japs. So do I. It is race prejudice, I guess. But I am
> strongly of the opinion that negros [*sic*] ought to be in Africa, yellow men
> in Asia and white men in Europe and America.[3]

At the same time, Truman regarded himself as a deeply religious man. He admired the ancient Hebrews, the people of the Bible, but he preferred the New Testament to the Old, and looked on the Bible primarily as a manual that provided a moral code for everyday behavior.[4]

In 1918, on his first visit to New York, on his way to embarking for the war in Europe, Truman added the Jews to his blacklist. Truman, now thirty-four years old, called the city a "kike town," and wrote to his first cousin, Mary Noland: "This town has 8,000,000 people, 7,500,000 of 'em are of Israelitish extraction. (400,000 are wops and the rest are white people)."[5]

Truman's friendship and short-lived business partnership with Eddie Jacobson has become the stuff of legend. Yet the two men were never intimate friends. Bess Truman never allowed Jacobson into their home—they met socially to play poker. When both men served in the same artillery unit during World War I—Truman being Jacobson's captain—the latter routinely took Truman's letters to his fiancée to the mailbox. Jacobson would have been shocked to read the contents of some of those letters. In February 1918, Truman boasted to Bess about the success of his army canteen: "I go count nickels and dimes up to four hundred dollars a day more or less. I guess I should be very proud of my *Jewish ability*."[6] (emphasis added)

Some might contend that these were the exuberant outpourings of an as-yet unsophisticated thirty-four-year-old. But the stereotypes Truman imbibed during his earlier years remained deeply embedded. Prejudicial comments of this nature, frequently quite gratuitous and usually confined to his private letters or diary, persisted throughout Truman's adult life. Just two examples from later years will be given here. In 1935, Senator Truman described to Bess a poker game in Washington, at which a Costa Rican minister had "screamed like a Jewish merchant."[7] In 1940, he informed Bess of his intention to fire a campaign worker, writing that he would "cut the smart Hebrew loose" as soon as he could.[8]

Truman's rancor against the Jews reached its apogee during the summer of 1947, just months before the historic UN vote to partition Palestine, which came at the end of November. On 21 July 1947, in a private diary entry, he released his bitter frustration following a ten-minute telephone conversation with Henry Morgenthau Jr., Roosevelt's Jewish secretary of the treasury. Truman wrote that Morgenthau had telephoned him about a "Jewish ship in Palistine [*sic*]."[9] The ship in question was evidently the *Exodus*, which had been forcibly boarded and towed to Haifa on 18 July. By 21 July, the ship's approximately 4,500 passengers were sailing on the high seas, being transported back to Europe in British ships. The Zionists had presumably mobilized Morgenthau to ask Truman to intervene with the British. At 6:00 pm on Monday, 21 July 1947, Truman wrote in his diary:

> He'd no business, whatever to call me. The Jews have no sense of proportion nor do they have any judgment on world affairs.
>
> Henry brought a thousand Jews to New York on a supposedly temporary basis and they stayed. When the country went backward—and Republican in the election of 1946, this incident loomed large on the D[isplaced] P[ersons] program.
>
> The Jews, I find are very, very selfish. They care not how many Estonians, Latvians, Finns, Poles, Yugoslavs or Greeks get murdered or mistreated as D[isplaced] P[ersons] as long as the Jews get special treatment. Yet when they have power, physical, financial or political *neither Hitler nor Stalin has anything on them for cruelty or mistreatment to the under dog.* Put an under dog on top and it makes no difference whether his name is Russian, Jewish, Negro, Management, Labor, Mormon, Baptist, he goes haywire. I've found very, very few who remember their past condition when prosperity comes.[10] (emphasis added)

The *Exodus* affair became a part of Zionist mythology. In 1958, Leon Uris wrote a novel based on it, which became the best-selling book since *Gone with the Wind*. Two years later, the film of the book, starring Paul Newman, became a box-office hit. The *Exodus* became the symbol of the struggle of the Jewish survivors of the Holocaust to build a Jewish state in Palestine. It was credited with having persuaded the United Nations to endorse their claim. However, with the recent discovery (in 2003) and publication of Truman's diary for 1947, it would appear that this particular myth now requires some revision.

The Jewish Factor in American Politics, 1945–1948

Clark Clifford, a Kansas City lawyer, was brought to the White House by Truman in 1946 and given the innocuous title of assistant naval aide. He became Truman's most influential political adviser, the man who gave direction to Truman's faltering presidency. On Zionist issues, Clifford relied largely on the briefs supplied to him regularly by Max Lowenthal, a Jewish lawyer Truman had met and befriended during the war. Lowenthal was never allotted a room of his own in the White House, but was given whichever office happened to be available. In effect, through the agency of Clifford, Lowenthal served as a direct liaison between the Zionists and the White House.[11]

On 19 November 1947, just ten days before the UN Resolution to partition Palestine into Arab and Jewish states, Clifford wrote a seminal memorandum on the importance and historical significance of the Jewish vote. The kernel of his argument ran:

> The Jewish vote, insofar as it can be thought of as a bloc, is important only in New York. But (except for Wilson in 1916) no candidate since 1876 has lost New York and won the Presidency, and its 47 votes are naturally the first prize in any election.[12]

Clifford's memorandum, which went on to supply statistics on the size of the Jewish communities in various states, spoke for itself: there was Pennsylvania with 36 votes, Illinois with 27, and Ohio with 23. Not only did these states have large Jewish populations, but the Jews there turned out to vote in high percentages. In the 1940s, candidates needed just 266 electoral votes in order to win the presidency.

The fact that Truman lost New York in the 1948 elections, but still went on to win the presidency, does not in any way detract from the importance the Truman White House attached to the Jewish vote, nor from the various ways in which individual Jews made vital contributions to Truman's own campaign and to the Democratic Party's election campaigns.

The Yom Kippur Statement, 4 October 1946

Perhaps the quintessential example of the role played by the Zionist lobby in American politics in the 1940s was the so-called Yom Kippur Statement issued by President Truman on 4 October 1946. The statement was interpreted generally (albeit incorrectly) as indicating his support for the establishment of a Jewish state in Palestine.[13]

Coming on the eve of the midterm congressional elections, Truman's speech was generally regarded at the time as a Democratic play for the Jewish vote. Both Truman and Secretary of State Dean Acheson went on record later as denying any ulterior political motives. In his memoirs, Truman claimed that there had been nothing at all unusual in his speech, and that it "just happened" to fall on the eve of Yom Kippur (the Jewish Day of Atonement). Acheson's record, published some twenty-three years later, is somewhat more circumspect. While denying that it was an election ploy, Acheson concedes, with hindsight, that it might have been of "doubtful wisdom."[14] However, the archives show quite clearly that the speech was indeed induced by the imminent elections.

Truman felt hounded by the Zionist lobby during the summer of 1946, in the weeks prior to the midterm congressional elections. He became embittered and infuriated by the stream of Democratic senators from New York, all urging him to support the Zionists' demand for a Jewish state in Palestine. On 27 July, after he had turned down previous requests, Truman agreed to receive two New York senators, James Mead and Robert Wagner, together with James McDonald, chairman of the sterile Anglo-American Committee on Palestine. Truman was short-tempered and impatient. When McDonald warned the president that his name would go down in history as anathema, Truman exploded: "Well, you can't satisfy these people.... The Jews aren't going to write the history of the United States or my history."[15]

McDonald reported back to the Zionists that Truman had "a mind-set which incapacitates him from understanding Jewish psychology."[16] Three days later, Truman was prevailed upon to receive a second delegation of congressmen, including the veteran Emmanuel Celler, representative for New York since 1923. Truman was again impatient, shuffling papers on his desk, interrupting constantly. Finally, in exasperation, he interjected: "This is all political. You are all running for re-election." He protested that he was tired of having Jews and Irishmen and Poles and Italians and Armenians come to him to further their own interests, and complained that he never heard anything from "Americans." He then rose from his seat and dismissed the delegation, stating that there was nothing further to discuss.[17]

At a cabinet meeting held the same day to discuss the various plans on the table for a solution to the Palestine impasse, Truman castigated the Jews. Henry Wallace recorded in his private diary that Truman said, "Jesus Christ couldn't please them when he was here on earth, so how would anyone expect that I would have any luck," and added his own comment: "[Truman] had no use for them and didn't care what happened to them."[18]

As was his habit, Truman ventilated his feelings to Bess. In a letter of 15 September, he wrote:

> Jim Mead came to see me about the New York campaign and then shot off his mouth as he went out of the front door. The Jews & the *crackpots* seem to be ready to go for Dewey. If they do, Jim is beaten and so he has to grasp for straws. There's no solution for the Jewish problem and

I fear the crackpots would turn the country over to Stalin if they had half a chance.[19] (emphases added)

The archival records reveal the circumstances of Truman's final capitulation to domestic political pressures (thereby exposing the "cosmetic" cover-up in both Truman's and Acheson's memoirs). On 3 October, Acheson gave the British ambassador in Washington advanced warning of the public statement that the president was about to make the next day, and made a lame attempt to explain the political exigencies that lay behind it.

> For the past several weeks Truman had been trying to keep Palestine out of domestic politics, but pressures had increased…. The administration understood that Governor Dewey [Republican] intended to make a major speech on the subject, and … Truman now felt it vital to make a statement.[20]

Ironically, the Democrats suffered large losses in the 1946 midterm elections. But with the elections behind him, Truman returned the Palestine issue to the State Department and rebuffed all further Zionist attempts to approach him. On 8 December 1946, at a private meeting with British Foreign Secretary Ernest Bevin, Truman explained how difficult it had been for him with the New York Jews and promised that now, with the elections over, he would be able to give the British a freer hand.[21]

1948: Presidential Politics and Elections

The removal of the Palestine issue from the domestic political agenda was all too short. In 1948, Truman faced the challenge of his first attempt to get elected president in his own right. The American political arena was plunged into what the State Department cynically referred to as the "silly season."

The UN Partition Resolution of 29 November 1947 had not brought tranquility to Palestine. A bitter civil war between Jews and Arabs broke out on the very next day. The State Department worked hard to revoke the Partition Resolution, before the Arab states became involved; it feared that a general conflagration in the Middle East would bring the intervention of the Soviet Union, thereby opening another front in the Cold War.

The Zionists had been monitoring events in Washington and at the UN headquarters at Lake Success. As early as January 1948, they had realized that U.S. policy on Palestine was once more back in the hands of the State Department. The Zionists appreciated accurately that the department's policy was to slow down the implementation of partition and, eventually, to abort it. They were told by Democratic Party officials that

> the top people in State and Defense don't care a thing about the elections. They are telling the President that if he has any courage at all, he will be willing to lose next Fall if that is the way to safeguard American security ... all this comes down to bases and oil and the whole problem of building up our position vis-à-vis Russia.[22]

The first open indication of an American retreat from partition came on 24 February 1948, when Warren Austin, the U.S. ambassador to the UN, told the Security Council that it was "authorized to take forceful measures with respect to Palestine to remove a threat to international peace," but "not to enforcing partition."[23]

The Zionists realized that another presidential intervention was required urgently. They mobilized Eddie Jacobson, Truman's army buddy from World War I, and his business partner both during and after the war. Jacobson had never in fact been a Zionist. Until 1947, when he was first recruited by the Zionists, he had never talked with Truman about either Jewish or Zionist issues. Once Truman reached the White House, Jacobson became a frequent visitor, accompanied usually by his lawyer-friend, Abe Granoff, another Kansas City Jew and a member of Truman's small poker-playing circle. Jacobson and Granoff would fly up to Washington from Kansas City without troubling first to check if the president could fit them into his schedule. Once they were ensconced in their Washington hotel, a telephone call to the White House infallibly secured them a reception the same day.[24]

The Zionists evidently secured an early warning about Austin's speech before the UN Security Council. In the early hours of 22 February 1948, Jacobson received a telephone call from Frank Goldman, a prominent American Zionist, asking him to approach the president to get him to agree to receive the aging veteran Zionist leader, Dr. Chaim Weizmann. Jacobson sent Truman an urgent telegram that same morning, but Truman refused to see Weizmann, insisting that there was nothing new Weizmann could possibly tell him.

At the urging of the Zionists, Jacobson flew up to Washington on 12 March. As usual, Truman received him on the same day. On the way in, Matt Connelly, Truman's appointments secretary, warned Jacobson not to discuss Zionism. Truman told his old friend why he had closed the White House doors to the Zionist lobby. He complained "how disrespectful and how mean certain Jewish leaders had been to him," how they had "slandered and libeled him." He had been especially upset by Rabbi Abba Hillel Silver, a Zionist of Republican persuasion, who had more than once raged in Truman's office, banged on his desk, and shouted at him. Therefore, he had instructed Connolly to refuse admission to all Zionists.[25]

Jacobson's intervention with Truman in March 1948 was indeed successful. But as Jacobson himself recalled later, during that visit, his "dear friend, the President of the United States," was "at that moment as close to being an anti-Semite as a man could possibly be." After some cursing, Truman finally agreed to receive the Zionist leader, Dr. Chaim Weizmann, largely as a personal favor to a lifelong friend, in whose debt he felt himself to be.[26]

Yet on the day after Truman received Weizmann at the White House and promised he would see partition through—when Truman was away on a short holiday—the State Department initiated a new proposal at the UN, proposing to shelve the partition resolution and set up a temporary UN trusteeship over Palestine until peaceful conditions were restored. The Zionists regarded this as a low betrayal.[27]

However, Jacobson never faltered in his personal loyalty to Truman, and Truman never forgot a friend. During Truman's famous whistle-stop election campaign in 1948, which turned the scales in his favor, Jacobson literally saved the president of the United States, more than once, from being thrown off the rented train. When Truman ran out of funds to pay for the next stage of the train journey, he would phone Jacobson for more funds. Jacobson would make a quick house-to-house collection from his Kansas City Jewish friends, and then fly up with the money to wherever the train was stopped, either with a check or with pockets full of cash.

Truman's Recognition of Israel, May 1948

On 12 May 1948, a secret meeting was held at the White House at which Truman tried to secure the agreement of Secretary of State Marshall to granting recognition to the State of Israel, which was due to declare independence forty-eight hours later. As he entered the room, Marshall objected furiously to the presence of Clark Clifford, Truman's political aide. Truman replied calmly that Clifford was present at the meeting because he, the president, had asked him to come. The State Department objected that there was no precedent for recognizing a state that did not yet have internationally recognized borders.

Clark Clifford presented two arguments in favor of prompt American recognition: first, the United States would preempt the Soviets, and second, early recognition would restore the president's position with his Jewish voters. Marshall protested vehemently: "This is straight politics." No one contradicted him.

Undersecretary of State Lovett countered that contrary to Clifford's political reasoning, American recognition would be highly detrimental to the prestige of the president and would be regarded as "a transparent attempt to win the Jewish vote."[28] Such a move would lose more votes than it would gain. The State Department insisted that they could not recognize Israel before the new state had even requested recognition. When the conference degenerated into an ill-tempered row about Truman's electoral prospects—with Marshall going so far as to threaten that he would not vote for the president in November—Truman called off the meeting abruptly, without having reached any decision.

Over the next thirty-six hours, Clifford, working behind the scenes, stage-managed the American recognition by orchestrating an Israeli request for recognition and by securing Marshall's agreement not to openly oppose the president. Quite clearly, the whole maneuver was motivated by political considerations, not least by the desire to recoup for the president the Jewish support that White House political advisers believed he had lost just two months before when the State Department had sponsored the trusteeship proposal at the UN.

The resulting scene at the UN General Assembly on 14 May was unprecedented general pandemonium. Warren Austin, head of the U.S. delegation, was advised by Dean Rusk, director of the office of United Nations Affairs, that the president was about to grant recognition to the new Jewish state. Austin was so upset and disgusted that he left the UN building without even informing his own delegation in the UN Assembly Hall of what was about to take place. The first news of Truman's recognition arrived over the UN ticker tape, leaving the American delegation red-faced with surprise.[29]

In a private letter written on 15 May, the day after his recognition of Israel, Truman made it clear that he would have preferred the 1946 recommendation of the Anglo-American Committee on Palestine—a unitary state, with minority rights for the Jews.[30]

Conclusion

President Truman's policy towards the Zionist struggle for a Jewish state was fraught with zigzags and inconsistencies that reflected the turmoil of a man who saw the logic in the State Department argument—that support of the Zionist cause could prove to be detrimental to the American national interest—but was driven, if not coerced, against his own judgment and feelings, by domestic political exigencies.

Notes

1. Miller, *Plain Speaking*, 183.
2. Harry Truman to Bess Wallace, 16 October 1911, in Ferrell, *Dear Bess*, 52.
3. Harry Truman to Bess Wallace, 22 June 1911, in ibid., 39; and published in the *Kansas City Star*, 10 April 1983.
4. See Miller, *Plain Speaking*, 214.
5. Truman to Mary Ethel Noland, 26 March 1918, in Mary Ethel Noland Papers, Box 1, HSTL. The term "kike," derived from "Isaac," is a derogatory term for Jews, and "wop" is a derogatory term for someone of Italian descent.
6. Harry to Bess, 3 February 1918, in Ferrell, *Dear Bess*, 242.
7. Harry to Bess, 30 June 1935, in ibid., 366.
8. Harry to Bess, 30 August 1940, in ibid., 443.
9. The entire desk diary for the year 1947, in Truman's own handwriting, has been transcribed and made available on the Internet (http://www.trumanlibrary.org/diary). In May 1945, while still serving as Treasury secretary, Morgenthau had, at the Zionists' behest, urged the newly inaugurated President Truman to set up a cabinet-level committee to deal with the Jewish DP problem; Cohen, *Truman and Israel*, 111.
10. Truman diary, entry for 21 July 1947, HSTL. Cf. Cohen, "New Look at Truman and 'Exodus 1947.'"
11. On Max Lowenthal's crucial role, see Cohen, *Truman and Israel*, 77–82. On Lowenthal's briefing of Clifford prior to the critical meeting at the White House on 12 May 1948, on whether the administration should grant immediate recognition to the new Jewish state, see Cohen, *Truman and Israel*, 209–11.
12. Clifford memorandum of 19 November 1947, Clifford Papers, Box 22, HSTL, cited in Cohen, *Truman and Israel*, 60.
13. In fact, Truman expressed his support for a reasonable compromise between the Zionists' demand for a Jewish state in a part of Palestine, and the British Provincial Autonomy plan; Cohen, *Truman and Israel*, 137–46.
14. Truman, *Memoirs: Years of Hope*, 153–54; and Acheson, *Present at the Creation*, 176.
15. Reports of meeting in Z5/1175, Z4/20276, CZA.
16. Report in Z5/1175, CZA.
17. Harry Spiro to Benjamin Akzin, Z5/1175, CZA. The delegation included eight Democrat congressmen and one Republican congressman, Leonard Hall. Celler was of mixed Catholic-Jewish descent.
18. Henry Wallace diary entry for 30 July 1946, in Blum, *Price of Vision*, 606–7.
19. Harry to Bess, 15 September 1946, in Ferrell, *Dear Bess*, 537.
20. Dean Acheson, interview with Ambassador Inverchapel, 3 October 1946, 867N.01/10-346, National Archives (US), cited in Cohen, *Truman and Israel*, 144–45.
21. Note of meeting, FO 800/513, National Archives (UK).
22. Gale Sullivan (vice chairman of Democratic National Committee) interview with Freda Kirchway, 4 February 1948, in *Political and Diplomatic Documents*, ed. Yogev, 297–98.
23. U.S. Dept. of State, *Foreign Relations of the United States, 1948*, 5. 2:651–54, cited in Cohen, *Truman and Israel*, 180.
24. On Jacobson, see Cohen, *Truman and Israel*, 8, 10–18, 74.
25. Cohen, *Truman and Israel*, 183–87.
26. Jacobson to Josef Cohn, 27 March 1952, Jacobson Papers, Correspondence files, HSTL, reproduced in *American Jewish Archives Journal* 20/1 (April 1968): 4–15; and quoted in Cohen, *Truman and Israel*, 186.

27. On the Trusteeship Proposal, see Cohen, *Truman and Israel,* 188–98.
28. McClintock memorandum, 12 May 1948, in U.S. Dept. of State, *Foreign Relations, 1948,* 5.2:972–76.
29. On the American recognition, see Cohen, *Truman and Israel,* 191–222.
30. Letter to Bartley Crum, 15 May 1948, in Cohen, *Truman and Israel,* 22.

Works Cited

Acheson, Dean. *Present at the Creation: My Years in the State Department.* New York: Norton, 1969.

Blum, John Morton, ed. *The Price of Vision: The Diaries of Henry A. Wallace.* Boston: Houghton Mifflin, 1973.

Cohen, Michael J. "A New Look at Truman and 'Exodus 1947.'" *Israel Journal of Foreign Affairs* 3.1 (Jan. 2009): 93–100.

———. *Truman and Israel.* Berkeley: University of California Press, 1990.

Ferrell, Robert H., ed. *Dear Bess: The Letters from Harry to Bess Truman, 1910–1959.* New York: Norton, 1983.

Miller, Merle. *Plain Speaking: An Oral Biography of Harry S. Truman.* New York: Berkley, 1974.

Sullivan, Gale. Interview by Freda Kirchway, 4 February 1948. In *Political and Diplomatic Documents, December 1947–May 1948,* edited by Gedalia Yogev, 297–98. Jerusalem: Israel State Archives/Israel Government Printing Office, 1980.

Truman, Harry S. *Memoirs: Years of Hope.* New York: Doubleday, 1956.

U.S. Department of State. *Foreign Relations of the United States, 1948.* Vol. 5 (2 pts.), *The Near East and Africa.* Washington, DC: U.S. Government Printing Office, 1975–76.

Archives

CZA   Central Zionist Archives, Jerusalem, Israel
HSTL   Harry S. Truman Library, Independence, Missouri, USA
National Archives (UK), London, UK
National Archives (US), Washington, DC, USA

Searching for Synthesis

Melvyn Leffler

THE PAPERS PRESENTED IN THIS VOLUME reveal the difficulty of interpreting Truman's decision to recognize Israel. This topic has been widely explored, and the Radoshes' 2009 book promises to be absorbing. One will then be able to compare their new book with Michael Cohen's 1990 book and it will be interesting to do so, as readers will be able to see the difficulties that historians face in weighing conflicting evidence.[1] However different in interpretation, these papers add a great deal of nuance and detail to what is a familiar story in the historical literature. And they do provide a basis for an overall synthesis.

I think it is important to realize the degree to which Truman was ambivalent about the recognition of Israel. He did waiver, and his decision was contingent. He was beleaguered by conflicting, yet sometimes reinforcing, religious, political, humanitarian, geopolitical, and strategic impulses. U.S. policy floundered because of a conflict between the views of the State Department, the Army, the Joint Chiefs of Staff, and the Defense Department on the one hand, and the views of Truman's political advisers and some of his friends on the other. Truman did appear inconsistent. Yet, I think, ultimately, one should realize that Truman was practical and sensible.

Also, it should be noted that Truman's policies after 1948—until the end of his presidency in January 1953—underscored his view that Israel had a right to exist and must exist. But equally important, Truman came to believe that Israel should accommodate the legitimate needs of Arab-Palestinians, and that Israel should live in harmony with its Arab neighbors.

To sum up the divergent impulses that led to Truman's recognition of Israel, one must understand that Truman did possess a religious evangelical belief. He believed there was a promised land for the Jews. Professor Kirkendall stressed this point and, although I do not altogether agree with the emphasis he puts on it, it is an important point. Truman did believe that there was a promised land—a promised land for the Jews. He did read the Bible frequently as a young person.

Michael Cohen disagrees and paints a much different picture. Cohen is absolutely right in saying that if you read Truman's diaries, memoranda, and letters, you will see that he used words like "kike" often—very often! But on the other hand, as Ambassador Brown emphasizes, Truman had numerous Jewish friends; Eddie Jacobson was not the only one. And Truman chose to rely on several Jewish aides in the White House, like Sam Rosenman, David Niles, and Max Lowenthal. Their role in the decision to recognize Israel was absolutely critical. In their essay and in their new book, Ron and Allis Radosh illuminate how important these personal contacts were. Of course, had Truman favored recognition without any doubt or reservation to begin with, the task of these Jewish advisers and Jewish friends would not have been quite so arduous.

Ron and Allis Radosh, moreover, also remind us that Truman could become furious with Jewish lobbyists. He detested Abba Silver and became extremely angry if pushed too far. In this respect, Michael Cohen points to one of Truman's most embarrassing diary entries as if it were a major revelation. But that diary entry is not a secret. Indeed, to the credit of the Truman Library, the former president's embarrassing quotation is widely known; anyone can see it: "The Jews," Truman said, "are very, very selfish." They want special treatment, he went on; yet when they have power, Truman said, they act no differently than Stalin or Hitler.[2] Yes, he said these things and they sound terrible. But we need to put these words in larger perspective: Truman was not an anti-Semite, as has sometimes been implied. However embarrassing his words, his friendships and his actions suggest that he was no bigot—but he was a provincial American from the heartland of the country.

Notwithstanding his intermittent furor with Jewish lobbyists, Truman was— and I agree here with Michael Cohen—altogether cognizant of the importance of the Jewish vote, Jewish financial support, and New York Jewish voters. Anyone who doubts these generalizations should go to Michael Cohen's book. He presents persuasive evidence supporting these points.[3]

Politics then pushed in the direction of recognition, as Michael Cohen argues. But geopolitics, strategy, and diplomacy sometimes pushed in a very different direction. State and Defense Department officials did not want to antagonize

Arab leaders. They did not want to jeopardize access to Middle East oil. They did not want to lose access to the Great Britian air base at Suez. They did not want to give the Soviets the opportunity to maneuver their way into the region by capitalizing on inept American diplomacy. These were the views of most of the State and Defense Department officials as well as the generals and admirals on the Joint Chiefs of Staff.

Truman, in fact, was buffeted this way and that way. He was not an ardent supporter of Israel, although he clearly and unequivocally supported Jewish immigration to Palestine. Mostly, Truman was bothered by this issue. He wished it would go away. He felt he had more important priorities. He wrote to one senator that he hoped the Palestine question would be settled by a federal autonomous state, not by partition. But the New York Jews, Truman said, destroyed this possibility.

In other words, Truman was irritated that the Jews would settle for nothing but partition. He was right. Therefore, we should be clear: Jewish actions in Palestine created the reality that Truman accepted. This is the point that Alon Kadish stresses in writing about events in Palestine between January and May of 1948.

The Jews in Palestine created the reality that Truman recognized. Truman wanted the Jews to settle for less. When they did not do so, and when the trusteeship idea floundered and got no real support from anyone except a few proponents in the State Department, recognition became the only sensible answer. Truman wrote to his friend Eddie Jacobson in February 1948: "The situation has been a headache to me for two and a half years. The Jews are so emotional, and the Arabs are so difficult to talk with, that it is almost impossible to get anything done here."[4] And a few days after recognition, Truman wrote to Dean Alfange: "The main difficulty with our friends, the Jews in this country, is that they are very emotional.... The President of the United States has to be very careful not to be emotional or to forget that he is working for 145 million [Americans],"[5] not just Jews.

What ultimately became rational, not emotional, from Truman's perspective, was the decision for recognition. It was politically expedient, but it was not just politically expedient. It was a humanitarian gesture, but not just a humanitarian gesture. Truman and his White House advisers also came to see that the geopolitical, economic, and strategic advantages of recognition outweighed the disadvantages. They did worry that recognition would antagonize Arabs. However, they worried even more that if the United States was slow to recognize Israel, the Soviets would do so nonetheless. As a result, the Soviets would make inroads into the Middle East at the expense of U.S. influence. In a 9 May White

House memorandum written by Lowenthal, proponents of recognition explicitly warned that the Soviets might recognize Israel first, and that belated U.S. action might seem "begrudging." They worried that a Zionist state, with its socialist principles, might become a vehicle for the Soviets to become influential in the Middle East.[6] The Kremlin, in fact, did want to make inroads into the region, as Professor Vladislav Zubok argues.

Overall, Truman would have preferred not to deal with the issue, but he had to deal with it. And ultimately, economic, geopolitical, humanitarian, and political variables reinforced one another. Although State Department and Defense Department officials remained unhappy, President Truman clearly felt that in recognizing Israel he was not only doing something that was politically expedient; he believed that he was also making a decision that accorded with his humanitarian sensibilities and with U.S. interests. Clifford, for example, argued persuasively to Truman that he should not worry that the United States would lose access to Middle East oil. The Arabs, Clifford said, needed to sell oil as badly as the United States and Western Europe needed to buy oil. In fact, this is the point that Avraham Sela makes when he writes about the weakness of the Arab states. They needed revenue and they had to sell their oil. The Americans understood these things. Therefore, they did not have to worry about losing access to Middle East oil, or so Clifford argued to Truman.[7]

Once he recognized Israel, Truman did not consistently support Israel. At times, he was disgusted with Israeli policies, and he deeply resented the pressure exerted on him by Jewish lobbyists. He was not indifferent to Arab hardships, protests, and demonstrations. In fact, during his second term, from 1949 to 1953, he sought to pursue a more balanced policy. First, he imposed an embargo on arms shipments to Israel and to the Arab states. He wanted the United States and its allies to sell armaments only for the preservation of domestic order. He allowed the sale to Israel of some ammunition and some aircraft, but not jets and not 75 mm guns. Second, Truman wanted to deal with the refugee problem. He initially favored repatriation, but he bowed to Israeli pressure. In April 1949, Truman talked "bluntly" to Chaim Weizmann and felt "disgusted" with Jewish treatment of the Arab refugees. He suspended the payment of a $49 million balance on an export-import loan (although later on he allowed small parts of it to be used).[8] Truman then delivered economic aid and relief, not just to Israel, but to the Arab states and to the refugees. The Pentagon and the United States Public Health Service sent doctors and sanitary engineers to the refugee camps. Truman himself was in favor, very much in favor, of these initiatives. He also supported the UN Economic Survey Mission. For fiscal year 1952, Truman actually signed an appropriations bill that called for $65 million for Israel and $65 million for Arabs, for the Arab states, and for the refugees.

Third, during his second administration, Truman sought ways to arrange a permanent settlement between the Arabs and the Jews in the Middle East. His initial proposals called for some Israeli territorial concessions. And in April 1950, his administration supported Jordanian annexation of the West Bank when the British threw their full support to Jordanian claims. But Truman never pressed his demands for additional Israeli territorial concessions. The domestic political costs were too high.

This experience illustrates that small nations have considerable ability to get their way, especially when they can exploit domestic politics inside the United States. They can leverage their influence most effectively when matters are not of primary importance to U.S. officials—and these matters were never of primary importance to Harry Truman.

Truman believed that lasting peace required equity. For him, it was not a matter of good versus evil, but of complexity and of contested legitimacy. He championed compromise and he called for mutual concessions. But he lacked fortitude, the political capital, and the diplomatic capabilities to force compromise. Furthermore, the Communist takeover in China in 1949, the Soviet Union's explosion of an atomic weapon that same year, and the North Korea invasion of South Korea in June of 1950 focused President Truman's attention in other parts of the globe.

In conclusion, Truman was not the unequivocal champion of Israel that he is often portrayed to be. He recognized Israel's right to exist when Israeli actions gave him little choice. But he felt that Israel had to act justly to dispossessed Arabs or peace would never come. He was frustrated, sometimes even embittered, by the intransigence of Arabs and Jews. In his eyes, they all seemed unreasonable.

Now, with the passage of time, Harry Truman's stature has risen greatly. His decision to recognize Israel and his aspiration for just treatment of dispossessed Arabs add to his stature. He was a president, like George W. Bush, who generally liked to see things in black and white. But although Truman often talked about good versus evil, Truman rarely, if ever, talked about Israeli-Arab affairs in this way. In the heart of the Middle East, in the land Truman believed God promised the Jews, he also knew the issues were of profound complexity.

 Melvyn Leffler

Notes

1. Radosh and Radosh, *A Safe Haven;* and Cohen, *Truman and Israel.*
2. Truman, 1947 diary, entry for 21 July, HSTL. Online at Harry S. Truman Library and Museum, "The Recognition of the State of Israel: Documents" (http://www.trumanlibrary.org/whistlestop/study_collections/israel/large/index.php?action=docs).
3. Cohen, *Truman and Israel.*
4. Truman to Jacobson, 27 February 1948, in Merrill, *Documentary History of the Truman Presidency.* Vol. 24, *United States and the Recognition of Israel,* 63.
5. Truman to Alfange, 28 May 1948, in Merrill, *Documentary History of the Truman Presidency.* Vol. 24, *United States and the Recognition of Israel,* 158.
6. Max Lowenthal, Memorandum dated 9 May 1948, HSTL. Online at Harry S. Truman Library and Museum, "The Recognition of the State of Israel: Documents" (http://www.trumanlibrary.org/whistlestop/study_collections/israel/large/index.php?action=docs).
7. Clark Clifford, memorandum, 8 March 1949, in U.S. Dept. of State, *Foreign Relations, 1949,* 6:694–95.
8. Hahn, *Caught in the Middle East,* 102.

Works Cited

Cohen, Michael. *Truman and Israel.* Berkeley: University of California Press, 1990.

Hahn, Peter L. *Caught in the Middle East: U.S. Policy Toward the Arab-Israeli Conflict.* Chapel Hill: University of North Carolina Press, 2004.

Merrill, Dennis, ed. *Documentary History of the Truman Presidency.* Vol. 24, *The United States and the Recognition of Israel.* Bethesda: University Publications of America, 1998.

Radosh, Ronald, and Allis Radosh. *A Safe Haven: Harry S. Truman and the Founding of Israel.* New York: Harper, 2009.

U.S. Department of State. *Foreign Relations of the United States, 1949.* Vol. 6, *The Near East and Africa.* Washington, DC: U.S. Government Printing Office, 1977.

Archives

HSTL   Harry S. Truman Library and Museum, Independence, Missouri

CONTRIBUTORS

Uri Bialer is professor of international relations at the Hebrew University of Jerusalem, where he has been for over thirty years. He earned a doctorate from the London School of Economics in 1974. He has been a research fellow at Oxford University and the British Academy, a visiting professor at the University of Chicago, and a senior research fellow at the Israeli Foreign Ministry. His books include *Cross on the Star of David: The Christian World in Israel's Foreign Policy, 1948–1967* (2005), *Oil and the Arab-Israeli Conflict* (1999), and *Between East and West: Israel's Foreign Policy Orientation* (1990).

William A. Brown served as U.S. Ambassador to Israel from 1988 to 1992. Prior to that, he served as U.S. Ambassador to Thailand; as Principal Deputy Assistant Secretary for East Asian and Pacific Affairs, U.S. Department of State; as Deputy Chief of Mission in Taipei, Taiwan, and in Tel Aviv, Israel; and in embassies and consular offices in Hong Kong, Singapore, Malaysia, Moscow, and New Delhi. He has a doctorate from Harvard University.

Michael J. Cohen is professor emeritus of history, Bar-Ilan University. His books include *Strategy and Politics in the Middle East, 1954–1960: Defending the Northern Tier* (2004), *Truman and Israel* (1990), *The Origins and Evolution of the Arab-Zionist Conflict* (1987), and *Churchill and the Jews* (1985).

Michael J. Devine is the director of the Harry S. Truman Library and the president of the Harry S. Truman Library Institute for National and International Affairs. He has also served as the director of the American Heritage Center at the University of Wyoming, as Illinois State Historian, and as director of the Illinois Historic Preservation Agency and the Illinois State Historical Society. He has a doctorate in history from Ohio State University. He is the author of *John W. Foster* (1981), and coeditor of two volumes in the Truman Legacy Series published by Truman State University Press, *The National Security Legacy of Harry S. Truman* (2005) and *Israel and the Legacy of Harry S. Truman* (2008).

Alon Kadish is professor of history at the Hebrew University of Jerusalem and senior research fellow at the Israeli Defence Force Centre for the Study of Tactics and Force Employment. He has a doctorate from the University of Oxford. He is the author of *The Oxford Economists in the Late Nineteenth Century* (1982), *Apostle Arnold: The Life and Death of Arnold Toynbee, 1852–83* (1986), and *Historians, Economists and Economic History* (1989).

Richard Kirkendall is Scott and Dorothy Bullitt Professor Emeritus at the University of Washington. His doctorate is from the University of Wisconsin. He is the editor of four books about the life and career of Harry S. Truman: *Harry's Farewell: Interpreting and Teaching the Truman Presidency* (2004), *The Harry S. Truman Encyclopedia* (1990), *The Truman Period as a Research Field: A Reappraisal, 1972* (1974), and *The Truman Period as a Research Field* (1967). He has had a long association with the Harry S. Truman Library and the Harry S. Truman Library Institute for National and International Affairs.

Melvin Leffler is Edward Stettinius Professor of American History at the University of Virginia. His doctorate is from Ohio State University. He is the author of *For the Soul of Mankind: The United States, the Soviet Union, and the Cold War* (2008), *The Specter of Communism: The United States and the Origins of the Cold War, 1917–1953* (1994), and *Preponderance of Power: National Security, the Truman Administration, and the Cold War* (1991). He is coeditor of the forthcoming three-volume *Cambridge History of the Cold War.*

Haim D. Rabinowitch is rector of the Hebrew University of Jerusalem. He served as acting academic director of the Harry S. Truman Research Institute for the Advancement of Peace from 2006 to 2008. A professor in the Hebrew University's Robert H. Smith Faculty of Agriculture, Food and Environment, he is one of the world's leading authorities on crop improvement. He received his doctorate from the Hebrew University of Jerusalem.

Allis Radosh and **Ronald Radosh** are the authors of *Safe Haven: Harry S. Truman and the Founding of Israel* (2009). Allis Radosh has taught at Sarah Lawrence College and the City University of New York, and has served as a program officer at the National Endowment for the Humanities. She also coauthored with Ronald Radosh *Red Star Over Hollywood: The Film Colony's Long Romance with the Left* (2005). Ronald Radosh is professor emeritus at the City University of New York and adjunct senior fellow at the Hudson Institute. His other books include *The Rosenberg File* (coauthor, 1983), *Commies: A Journey through the Old Left, the New Left and the Leftover Left* (2001), and *The Amerasia Spy Case: Prelude to McCarthyism* (1996).

Avraham Sela is A. Ephraim and Shirley Diamond Professor of International Relations at Hebrew University, Jerusalem, where he earned his doctorate, and senior research member at the Harry S. Truman Research Institute for the Advancement of Peace. He is the coauthor of *The Palestinian Hamas: Vision, Violence and Adjustment* (2000 and 2006), the author of *The Decline of the Arab-Israeli Conflict: Middle East Politics and the Quest for Regional Order* (1998), and the editor of *The Continuum Political Encyclopedia of the Middle East* (rev. ed., 2002).

Gabriel Sheffer is professor of political science at the Hebrew University of Jerusalem. His doctorate is from the University of Oxford. He has served as the director of the Jerusalem Group of National Planning at the Jerusalem Van Leer Foundation, and the Leonard Davis Institute for International Relations. He performed research for David Ben-Gurion and has worked as a consultant for the Office of the Israeli Prime Minister and the Israeli Foreign Ministry, Ministry of Defense, and Ministry of Education. He is the author of *Moshe Sharett, Biography of a Political Moderate* (1996) and of *Diaspora Politics: At Home Abroad* (2003), and coauthor of *Who Leads? On Israeli-Diaspora Relations* (2006).

Allen Weinstein served as Archivist of the United States from 2005 to 2008. From 1985 to 2003 he was president of the Center for Democracy in Washington, DC. Dr. Weinstein received his doctorate in history from Yale University and taught at Smith College, Boston University, and Georgetown University. His many publications include *The Haunted Wood: Soviet Espionage in America—Stalin Era* (1999). In 1986, he was awarded the United Nations Peace Medal and he twice received the Council of Europe's Silver Medal (1990 and 1996) for his humanitarian work.

Vladislav Zubok is associate professor of history at Temple University and research fellow at the National Security Archive, George Washington University. His doctorate is from the Institute for U.S. and Canadian Studies of the Academy of Sciences, Moscow. He is the author of *Zhivago's Children: The Last Russian Intelligentsia* (2009) and *A Failed Empire: The Soviet Union in the Cold War from Stalin to Gorbachev* (2007), and the coauthor of *Anti-Americanism in Russia: From Stalin to Putin* (2000) and *Inside the Kremlin's Cold War: From Stalin to Khrushchev* (1996).

Ronald W. Zweig is Marilyn and Henry Taub Professor in Israel Studies, professor of Hebrew and Judaic studies, and director of the Taub Center for Israel Studies at New York University. From 1983 to 2004, he was professor of history at Tel Aviv University. His doctorate is from the University of Cambridge. He is the author of *Britain and Palestine during the Second World War* (1986), *German*

Reparations and the Jewish World: A History of the Claims Conference (2001), and *The Gold Train: The Looting of Hungarian Jewry* (2002); he is the coauthor of *Escape through Austria: The Flight of Jewish Survivors from Eastern Europe, 1945–1948.*

Index